SPEAK OUT!
while Public Speaking

How to Sound and Look Great to Influence, Win your Audience and Sell More. Feel Confident, Persuade and Deliver your Best Authentically while On-Stage, On-Camera, and during Business Presentations and Meetings

LORNA EARNSHAW

Copyright @2018 Lorna Earnshaw
All rights reserved
ISBN-10: 1987674030
ISBN-13: 978-1987674033

DEDICATION

For Mamá and la Abuela, always with me. For my teachers Liliana Parafioriti and Silvia Goldberg, and for all my students.

CONTENTS

	Introduction	Pg 5
1	Chapter 1: How to Stay Connected	Pg 12
2	Chapter 2: Your Voice	Pg 40
	a) Vocal Troubleshooting	Pg 41
	b) The 5 steps to a Powerful Voice	Pg 78
3	Chapter 3: Your Non-verbal Communication	Pg 98
4	Chapter 4: Your Word Choice and Word Performance	Pg 115
	Prologue	Pg 140

INTRODUCTION: WELCOME TO SPEAK OUT!

If your presentation skills are not good enough, your audience will unconsciously assume that your work, product or even your professional skills are poor as well.

I know exactly how it feels when you have so much to say but you seem to have a hard time finding the right words. Suddenly, your mind starts drifting and unwanted thoughts take you away from the moment. You are worried about how your presentation is going. You are wondering if you look okay and what the audience thinks about you. You are trying way too hard to make a good impression.

You might be speaking at an event, giving a speech or an interview, or pitching a new project during an important business meeting with your prospects.

In any case, in just one moment, your focus is gone. Your body starts feeling uncomfortable and you get nervous. It is painful. Maybe you sweat or get a dry mouth. Maybe your voice becomes shaky and you need to clear it

Get the FREE VIDEO TRAINING at

http://www.lornavocals.com/p/speakoutbonus

up constantly. You silently pray that this is over soon, and you wonder if your audience is noticing your anxiety.

After the presentation is done, even if people seem to like your work, you feel that your talk could have been better.

If what I have just mentioned describes your current performance, this book is for you. My goal is to help you speak out (!), so that you can taste how sweet it feels to succeed and deliver your message powerfully.

How would it be if you could experience freedom and fulfillment on stage? In those instants, you will feel suspended in the beautiful bliss of the moment. You will be completely present and expressing your highest self. Your voice will be powerful and you will own it. The stage will be your territory. You and the audience will be in fantastic synchronicity.

Afterwards, you will leave the stage with a sense of mission accomplished and inner peace. You will have no doubt that you had shared the best of you and that you had enriched yourself and other people's lives in the process.

Being honest, I have already been on both sides: being uncomfortable during my early stages and, later on, feeling powerful once I have overcome my challenges. That is why I promise you that you can also cross that bridge. I have helped thousands of people to free their voices in the past 15 years, and I went through that process myself when I learned how to sing from scratch and became a professional singer-songwriter and vocal coach.

In this book, I intend to share with you the result of more than 30 years of experience being on-camera, on-stage and also behind the scenes improving artist's and speaker's performance.

My story

At 10 years-old, I went on TV for the first time when I participated in a singing contest for kids in Argentina, my home country. That was not a pleasant initiation at all. I got extremely nervous and insecure. However, little by little, I got used to being on the spot and, later on, I did some acting work on commercials and TV shows.

At 20 years-old, I started working as a professional Classical Egyptian dancer and instructor, and the following year I graduated in Journalism. At that time, I had been studying at the National Conservatory of Music for years. At 24 years-old, I started performing professionally, singing and playing piano.

The following years, I performed five nights a week as a musician and as professional Classical Egyptian Dancer.

In 2003, I initiated my work as a singing instructor. Since then, I have been working as a vocal coach, teaching privately and lecturing about the subject in more than 200 workshops and webinars in English, Spanish and Portuguese.

In 2013, I moved to Los Angeles, got my Bachelor's Degree in Songwriting, started my vocal studio in Hollywood and released new online educational products.

Since then, I have worked consistently with online marketing for my own business, while I have also advised others on how to grow their own online presence and improve their speaking skills.

During this period, while I was running my campaigns and creating my social media content with great success and a growing audience, I noticed that most of my fellow online entrepreneurs were struggling and not developing as fast as I did.

It was easy for me to speak and to be on video, to produce Facebook live broadcasts with many live viewers and to run highly converting webinars. I shot videos very fast, usually in one take, and without breaking a sweat. I looked self-confident and energetic. My followers loved me and they were buying from me like crazy!

Get the FREE VIDEO TRAINING at

http://www.lornavocals.com/p/speakoutbonus

Of course my ability to perform on-camera and on-stage and my capacity to connect with an audience and influence did not develop in one day. My results came after decades of investment in my education, which combines formal studies (two university diplomas) and years of artistic work as a singer-songwriter and vocal coach, and as a former dancer and dance instructor.

A world of new opportunities

Currently, I spend my days teaching in three languages: English, Spanish and Portuguese. The Internet has broken down frontiers and has expanded exponentially the possibilities of growth of businesses, artists and thought leaders. Since I realized the size of these opportunities, I have been passionate about exploring them and I have taken advantage of the available technology by online coaching people from all over the world while sitting at my desk at my Hollywood studio.

Nowadays, social media is a huge opportunity to start new avenues of income and to build audiences in a proportion that has never even been imaginable in the history of human kind.

Today, it is extremely easy and affordable for the common individual in the Western World to broadcast from his phone and start his own show. Companies create closer bonds with their customers by investing substantial budgets to hire social media celebrities, the so-called "influencers" who promote their products.

Speaking has become one of the most profitable activities, while online videos are being used to sell millions of dollars. In order to survive, every business needs to go online or at least to consider an online strategy in order to adjust to the new rules of the game.

Get the FREE VIDEO TRAINING at
http://www.lornavocals.com/p/speakoutbonus

In the current context in which video is considered the most efficient way to advertise and increase brand awareness, speaking has become one of the most valuable skills for those who have a message to share.

Communication can happen through several channels and it has never been so easy and cheap. On the other hand, the excess of information that is being sent out constantly and that stimulates our senses is way more than we can ever absorb. The attention span is being reduced to 8 seconds and now, more than ever, we need to improve our strategy to get our audience's attention while competing with millions of stimuli that is bombarding us constantly.

Many times, we have just one single opportunity to make a strong impression and to deliver our message. This delivery needs to be powerful, otherwise it will be forgotten easily and it might not impact our audience as we first intended to.

The sad thing is that many times, while a real treasure of talent is hiding beneath the surface, most of the people have not developed their speaking skills. These are those who are holding themselves back and who have a hard time presenting their message powerfully.

Studies have revealed that more than 75% of the population suffers from some kind of anxiety or stage fright before speaking in public. Therefore, we can conclude that speaking rarely comes as a natural ability and that, unfortunately, it is not a priority within the standards of traditional education.

How to breakthrough and Speak out!

As a vocal coach and as an artist, I know how important it is to develop your skills through serious training and practice. I have experienced beautiful growth myself and I have observed it in my colleagues and students af-

---

Get the FREE VIDEO TRAINING at

http://www.lornavocals.com/p/speakoutbonus

ter applying some of the tools and techniques I am sharing with you in this book.

Many of them came to me hopeless and frustrated. My job has been to help them dream again and to find the strategies to bring out the best they have to offer the world.

Just like I did and as my students were able to do it, I can assure you that you are capable of developing your talent towards becoming a powerful presenter too!

My approach combines the strong foundation of my formal studies as a journalist and as a singer-songwriter and vocal coach, with the online marketing techniques I have practiced as an online entrepreneur and marketing consultant. I will share with you how to connect with your audience with emotion and from your heart. That is where your true power resides!

In this book, I will explain the four pillars that will help you communicate efficiently and deliver a persuasive and integrated message.

We will focus on your voice, your non-verbal communication and your word choice, while strengthening an honest connection with your mission and your audience. Of course, this is just an introduction to the subject, and I could write a 200-page book for each one of the four principles I have just mentioned.

Nevertheless, considering the visual and audible nature of our topic, I would rather teach you the step-by-step on video or in person, in a more practical way in order to demonstrate examples and exercises. If you are interested, this book can be the first step before we work together through other platforms, or even in person!

I offer a variety of solutions to train and consult through live and online events, corporate speaking, one-on-one coaching and online courses.

Get the FREE VIDEO TRAINING at

http://www.lornavocals.com/p/speakoutbonus

Access my FREE video training as a special bonus for this book and start practicing RIGHT NOW!
Get the video lessons here:
http://www.lornavocals.com/p/speakoutbonus

Also, you can always leave me a review at my Facebook Page: Lorna. (http://www.facebook.com/pages/lornaeofficial

I wish with all my heart that this book will help you overcome whatever blockage there is to your free expression and your capacity to create a bigger impact.
Speak out! The world needs to hear!
Love,

Lorna

Get the FREE VIDEO TRAINING at

http://www.lornavocals.com/p/speakoutbonus

CHAPTER 1: HOW TO STAY CONNECTED.
Be yourself, speak from your heart and impact lives

How to look and sound more confident and authoritative during your presentations?

There is no way to fake authority. There is no way to fake self-confidence. Even if you rehearse the trickiest words. Even if you study NLP, sales techniques or advanced marketing strategies.

When you are in front of an audience, your emotions, your thoughts, and even your deepest secrets will unconsciously send out a signal that will be the ultimate message people will receive.

Unfortunately (or fortunately), there is no recipe or script that I can share with you that will make this challenge go away.

If you want to be authoritative, you need to embrace your responsibility to lead others by providing guidance and value.

When you are teaching, speaking in public or performing, the more you focus on yourself, your needs and your interests, the more nervous and disconnected you will feel. It is all about communication, and this communication will flow more naturally as you give the best out of yourself, so that you can be a positive influence to your audience.

Once you take the time to deeply appreciate every single person listening to you, the opportunity to stand in front of them, and you concentrate on delivering your message with the ultimate goal of helping them, you will forget about being nervous! You will feel inspired and your positive feelings of appreciation and generosity will get you closer to them.

In case you are not repeating a fixed script, you will find the right words. In case you are performing a defined previous text, you will be able to pour your emotion so that your audience will be magnetized to you. That is what real authority is about!

Once, I was invited to participate in a Brazilian voice online summit. I was one of the featured renown speakers to teach about singing technique and I received the call to broadcast on live video from Los Angeles.

I carefully prepared my slides and my presentation in advance in order to cover the content that I had found to be of interest to my online followers and clients. At the time, these were both professional and amateur singers. I started the live video broadcast with around a hundred viewers. As I usually do in these type of events, I asked about the participants' experience and current challenges.

To my surprise, 90 per-cent of the audience were vocal coaches, speech therapists and there was even a significant number of Ear, Nose and Throat doctors. For a moment, I was paralyzed. My usual presentation includes the explanation of the process of phonation and basic vocal technique. Obviously, the participants of this particular online conference were already familiar with this type of information, because they were already educated voice professionals.

Get the FREE VIDEO TRAINING at
http://www.lornavocals.com/p/speakoutbonus

If I had moved forward with the presentation as I had planned in advance, it would have been a complete disappointment to the participants, because the content would have seemed way too basic for them. Therefore, I made a bold decision. I shut down my slides presentation and I improvised all the way through by changing the perspective of my topic.

Instead of teaching how to sing better, I approached the subject of "how to help your clients to use their voices more efficiently". I shared the best pedagogy secrets I had developed after being a vocal instructor for more than twelve years at the time. I decided to teach on this topic, since I had observed the poor methodology and mindset that other voice teachers (my colleagues) usually implemented. During my years as a voice coach, I had taught students who were previously working with other coaches and who would come to me very frustrated because of the poor result they got. Many of them even had a wrong mindset and an erroneous approach to our field of study.

Back to my live conference, I decided to talk about mindset, pedagogy and methodology to help clients and students overcome their vocal challenges. This change was an absolute success!

The participants got a lot of value and knowledge that would enrich their practices, while some of the viewers who were not voice professionals, but only aspiring singers, learned much as well and were impressed by me, because I was actually teaching other professionals how to help students or clients themselves.

After that improvised presentation, I reinforced my image as an authority to the participants' eyes. I was able to provide value to my listeners just by focusing on what they needed of me in that moment.

If I had focused on myself and in my insecurities, it would have been a disaster! I could have thought: "Oh my God! What am I going to do now? These are highly educated listeners, they already know everything I am about to teach! They will think I am not that good and they will leave. I will look terrible!" Maybe I would have felt paralyzed and insecure if I had simply followed up with my previous plan and the slides I had prepared. By focusing on the best that I had to share with them, we established a real connection and I was seen as an authority!

If you want to look and sound authoritative, be a leader! Your audience is looking for that leadership. During your presentation, they are giving you the opportunity to spend time with them and they are expecting you to conduct the act. Chances are that they are willingly sitting in front of a stage or watching you on social media because they are expecting to get some kind of value in exchange. Nobody goes to a speaking event to get disappointed in case the talk is not good, and nobody goes out to a recital or to the theater secretly wishing for the performer to fail.

After being on stages for more than 30 years, I found out that the more I own the opportunity of being on stage, and the more I embrace my responsibility to take care of my audience, the more naturally I am able to perform according to my real full potential.

If you have something to share during your presentation, the more you are aware of the importance of delivering your message, and the positive impact you are capable of creating, the more authoritative you will appear to the eyes of your public.

They need your leadership. We all need to be influenced by experts and performers that will enrich our experiences and bring in solutions for our problems or add value to our lives.

If you are delivering a sales presentation, your success will depend on how you can influence your audience to take action and acquire your product. Hopefully, if the proposal is ethical, your product will be beneficial to them and, while generating profit for you, it will also benefit your clients.

Get the FREE VIDEO TRAINING at

http://www.lornavocals.com/p/speakoutbonus

When you really believe in whatever you have to offer and you are aware of how this information or art performance will ultimately be beneficial for both sides, you have the ultimate weapon of persuasion in your hands.

Have you ever recommended a product that you love to a friend or even left a review to encourage others to buy something that has really worked out for you? If so, then you already know how it feels to speak about a solution when you are owning your authority! In that case, your opinion will be relevant to others, since you are one of the people who have the experience of being a client, while you are sharing your opinion in order to help others make a decision!

When you are in front of an audience, your authority on stage will be the result of your connection to your mission. Whenever you get nervous thinking about what people will think of you while you are presenting, you will get disconnected from your highest self and from your audience. That disconnection will take place when you are just worried about yourself and your ego.

When I started working as a singing instructor, and even before, when I was a dance teacher, I learned the meaning of service in my life. For some reason, I noticed that I felt way more comfortable performing for my students in class, even in short presentations, than while I was singing or dancing on stage.

I noticed that while teaching, I was capable of focusing completely on my students. It was not about me looking good and impressing others. It was about helping them achieving their dreams so that they could express themselves through art, just like I was able to.

Therefore, I felt compelled to come up with creative ways of explaining how to perform certain techniques and movements. This required a great effort from my part. I needed to extensively analyze things that were completely natural for me at that point so that I could create a framework to teach.

As an experienced professional, I did not need to analyze what I was doing in order to perform a certain dance step or to sing a melody with some specific vocal technique. Nevertheless, my responsibility was to deconstruct the movements and to find a way to allow my students to achieve the same results that I did. My success and my reward for being a good teacher consisted on helping them get results and look good.

There was a specific day when I really understood the responsibility of being a teacher and how careful I needed to be when presenting my content and influencing my students. Even if this was applied to a situation with a private lesson in which I was teaching just one person for an hour, it really opened my eyes so that I could finally understand the superior mission I had in my hands.

I was going through a tough time in my life. I had a very bad experience with an "agent" who took advantage of me. I was working hard on my career as a singer-songwriter and I had this person represent me. I believed he could help me finally have the breakthrough I was looking for. After working with this person for more than a year and a half I found out that I – along with more than a hundred people who had supported my musical project at the time – was a victim of a scam performed by this so-called agent/musical producer.

After I discovered this betrayal, I found myself without work, without money and, worst of all, grieving over my crashed dreams. Because I had believed in this scammer, I had given up other professional opportunities in order to invest in my career as a singer following his advice. I had got the attention and investment of people who had supported the project, but after 18 months of hard work, we sadly found out that the whole thing was based on a lie.

Get the FREE VIDEO TRAINING at

http://www.lornavocals.com/p/speakoutbonus

In order to survive, I had to move to another city (I was living in Brazil at the time). Fortunately, I found a part-time job at a wonderful music school in the city of Porto Alegre (Escola Estação Musical), where I had a couple of private students.

I was depressed and ashamed of myself. I felt like a failure. I felt that I had been stupid and naive for believing the lies I had been told for a such a long time.

One day, I woke up and I could not stop crying. However, I needed to get ready to teach my student. I called my brother. Since I lost my mom at 25 and I never had a close relationship with my father, my brother Douglas had always been my main emotional support. He is a lawyer and worked at the court for almost 30 years in Buenos Aires, Argentina.

When my brother picked up the phone, I was crying. I told him that I was depressed and lonely. I was lost. I told him I had to go and teach a student but I did not feel capable enough because I was a mess.

Then, with an authoritative voice, he said: "You have a responsibility. Your obligation is to teach this person. It is not about you, it is about him! He has been waiting the whole week for this class, and you do not even know how hard it is for him to pay you. He is heading now to see you to try and see if MAYBE he can learn a little bit of everything you know. You do not have the right to be a mess right now. Take a shower, put your makeup on and do your job by giving this guy the best singing class he could ever get".

I just said okay. Suddenly, I did not feel like a victim anymore. I stopped whining about what had happened to me. I felt grateful for my knowledge on vocal technique and that I had a job. I felt grateful because my student believed so much in me that he paid for a month of lessons in advance.

I took a shower and I stopped crying. I got ready and I walked to the music school. I looked great and I met my student. I gave him an excellent class. I do not remember exactly the words that I said. I just remember the feeling

---

Get the FREE VIDEO TRAINING at

http://www.lornavocals.com/p/speakoutbonus

of mission accomplished when the 50 minutes of our session were over. I was happy. I felt fulfilled because I had been able to teach him and to share everything I believed in. Despite my circumstances at the time and whatever tragic events had recently happened in my career as a singer, I felt deep inside of me that there was a constant invaluable treasure filled with everything I knew and believed about music. It was this passion that moved me to practice for hours when I was a child. It was the resilience that pushed me to find teachers as a teenager, even when I felt I was not talented enough.

From that beautiful and peaceful place inside my heart, by teaching that class, I was able to regain my authority. I had the responsibility to make my client's time and the money he spent on me worth it. That sense of obligation as a leader gave me the strength to do my job.

During that simple class, the right words flew out of my mouth beautifully. I sang, and my voice was as emotional as it had been during performances I had done in front of thousands of people at sold-out theaters.

This time, during this simple class, I felt relieved. I was not whining about my misadventure anymore. I actually had forgotten about it. I felt strong, I felt alive.

From that day on, I completely changed the way I had seen my activities as a teacher. The thought that it was about THEM (my students/listeners) and not about ME, was liberating. From that day on, I felt a deep love and compassion every time I was presenting myself. Then, the size of the audience or the circumstances of the event were secondary.

After that, I changed my approach to the way I was communicating with my clients and that had been my mindset for each one of my presentations. It could be for one person, for a small business group, for a hundred viewers on my webinars or from stage.

Get the FREE VIDEO TRAINING at

http://www.lornavocals.com/p/speakoutbonus

Since then, my clientele started growing. Even if I have always charged around 80 percent more than the rest of the voice coaches in town, my list of clients got bigger and bigger, and thanks to the word of mouth and videos I posted on YouTube, I got so busy I needed to open a waiting list. I gave masterclasses and workshops in several stages in different cities of Brazil. I felt excited about the opportunity to share my truth with those who were in the audience. I was in the moment. I could be funny and I could deliver high quality content by feeling powerful on stage. I could feel love and appreciation for those who were listening to me. That inspired me to try my best to share with them everything I know, without holding back. Those live events always resulted in many new clients who would approach me afterwards to have private sessions. One of them is Mauricio Giller, from Curitiba, who became my student in 2008 after one of my live presentations from stage and who had been studying with me consistently for more than ten years! Even nowadays, he still has two sessions per month with me via Skype, since now I live in Los Angeles!

I guess every performer has heard, at least once, the expression "show must go on", which is the main phrase of one of the band Queen's biggest hits. We all have heard stories of musicians, actors, politicians and many speakers who had to go on stage even at very tough moments in their lives. Some of them had recently lost a loved one, and some were going through tremendous stress for other reasons.

However, they only found the strength to move on when they focused on their audience and set their own personal needs aside.

In order to be a powerful presenter, you need to be focused on your audience and in the importance of delivering your message to each one of them. When you are connected to your mission, you will forget about your nervousness and you will own your authority.

Get the FREE VIDEO TRAINING at

http://www.lornavocals.com/p/speakoutbonus

Being in the moment vs self-talk

Living in Hollywood, you can easily get the opportunity to watch stand-up comedy shows with new talents or artists who are not very famous, while they hustle to make it to the biggest stages.

One day, my friend and hilarious comedian Allan Cunningham (http://www.turnuptheac.com) invited me to go with him to one of the bars where comedians "work out and network". He is a veteran in this modality, and anybody can tell that he is very confident on stage. I asked him why he was going to this place to perform for free along with a lot of beginners. He explained to me that it was an opportunity to keep practicing and to test new jokes, to see what works and what does not.

I was curious, and even though it was a rainy Monday night, I decided to go. In this bar on Sunset Boulevard, there was a small stage and around ten tables with an average of three chairs each. Even so, most of these chairs were empty.

There were about 15 comedians sitting on stools around the bar and talking as a group of old friends. One by one, they started taking the stage. Each of them had ten minutes to try their best. As a vocal coach, I started analyzing how effective each performance was. It was a challenging set up. Even if they were working hard, it was difficult to get a response from such a small audience, considering most of them were fellow comedians. It was therefore easy to compare each one's performance and the results they were getting.

One of them was visibly nervous. He was young, in his early twenties. While he performed the script he had prepared, I could tell he was way too worried about what people were thinking about him. Maybe his jokes were good. Honestly, I could not pay attention to most of what he said. My maternal instinct and my call as a voice coach spoke louder. I got nervous be-

Get the FREE VIDEO TRAINING at

http://www.lornavocals.com/p/speakoutbonus

cause he was nervous. I felt bad for him. Sometimes, I even pretended I was laughing, just to support him a little bit since there were just a few people reacting positively to his presentation. I got completely distracted and I could not pay attention to what he was saying! I definitely could tell he was a beginner.

Later on, another guy showed up, grey-haired and walking firmly to grab the microphone from the stand. He stayed quiet and stared at us for a while. He was having fun already! He started by making a couple of funny faces. People started laughing. He enjoyed that first reaction. He had already won the audience in the first minute of his presentation.

I could tell he was an experienced artist. He was having fun with us. I could feel the joy he experienced every time we laughed. He continued telling jokes and stories, while engaging the audience as part of the act. I felt relaxed and at ease. I did not have to worry. It was a relief that I did not have to fake my laugh or feel bad because the house was empty, which was the way I felt like during the inexperienced comedian's set.

The guy with the grey hair (the experienced comedian) was in the moment. He was present. He was not worried about his performance! He was just BEING. Just as you could be BEING and in the moment while meditating. If you are not familiar with meditation practices, this might sound a little way too metaphysical for you. Maybe you were expecting me to share only some rational tips or psychological techniques that will work so that you look professional.

Nevertheless, after more than 30 years of being engaged in different types of performing and artistic activities, I have learned that the more I have worried and the harder I have tried to look good and professional, the less I have succeeded. The more I have left aside my technical perfectionism by just relaxing so that I could experience the connection with my true self, the best I have been able to perform.

Get the FREE VIDEO TRAINING at

http://www.lornavocals.com/p/speakoutbonus

I highly recommend to anybody who is interested in improving their life and mental health, to establish a daily meditation practice. Meditation has proven results that enhance our focus and the balance of our emotions. By practicing 15 minutes per day, for at least 30 consecutive days, you will learn about the difference between the agitated activity of your mind, which is the origin of your fear, and who you really are. When you focus on your breathing, close your eyes and stay silent, you are practicing a connection with your higher self, and you learn to recognize your thoughts as circumstances that change constantly, while your essence and your inner stability stay constant and peaceful, like your breath.

I invite you to take a meditation challenge with me! It does not matter what your religion is or if you do not have a religion at all. Meditation has been scientifically proved as one of the best ways to improve the performance of our rational thinking, balance our emotions, create well-being and even to increase grey matter of the brain. It has been proven that consistent meditation increases the cortical thickness in areas related to paying attention.

Brief meditation exercise to do before your presentation

Testimonial:

"I was so lucky I got to meet Lorna and I got to work with her 1 on 1. Her visualization exercise got me so much more relaxed before I had to speak last week. The difference was unbelievable. In turn, I got to share it with several other speakers when I got to EmCee for other presenters the day after. Now I am working on breathing techniques and am excited about the next steps!" (Yvette Sonneveld, Netherlands- Inbound Marketing Trainer, Mentor & Consultant at Create Content With Confidence)

When we start our presentation, we step on the stage, in the meeting room or even when we go on camera, bearing the thoughts and conditioning that

---

Get the FREE VIDEO TRAINING at

http://www.lornavocals.com/p/speakoutbonus

we have been carrying around during the previous hours. Nevertheless, in the last minute, even if we have been practicing and we think we have prepared correctly, the fire alarm of fear might turn on and make us lose our balance.

The last minutes before the show starts can be painful and stressful. There is a peak of adrenaline and our bodies will respond to the high demand in order to generate extra energy and perform at our best capacity.

This is why I have created a simple exercise for my clients to practice before going on stage. It is the exercise I taught Yvette, whose testimonial I included at the beginning of this section.

It is intended to reconnect you with your mission and with whom you really are. It will work to gently calm your mind down, so that it can cooperate instead of trying to make you quit and go home.

1. Before your presentation, find a place where you can sit quietly for a couple of minutes.
2. Close your eyes.
3. Breath in through your nose and breath out through your mouth. You will learn how to do this in the abdominal breathing exercise I included in the next chapter of this book.
4. Remember what your mission is and why you are doing it. Imagine all the great things that you will accomplish as the result of this presentation. Pay attention to each one of those outcomes and feel the positive sensations that these thoughts bring to your body.
5. Picture someone that you have helped in the past. It could be one of your clients that has benefited from your work. Remember their words of gratitude towards you. Feel the appreciation for the opportunity of helping them. Feel the happiness because you have met them and be-

---

Get the FREE VIDEO TRAINING at

http://www.lornavocals.com/p/speakoutbonus

cause they trusted you. Think about the leap of faith you had to take in order to allow this encounter to take place.
6. Enjoy the moment of thinking and feeling these wonderful memories.
7. Open your eyes only when you are ready. Now you can start your presentation.

Download the audio version of this exercise as a guided meditation. Access for free http://www.lornavocals.com/p/speakoutbonus

Stage fright

I will confess that sometimes I have a tendency to be "in my head". Here is when, in the middle of a presentation, instead of feeling the passion and the excitement of having the opportunity to exercise my creativity, my mind starts making judgements about the situation. This is what happens if I am singing and I get worried that I am not sounding good enough, or that something might go wrong. Then I start getting even more anxious because I notice I am nervous. Then, my mouth gets dry, my hands get sweaty. I have even been in a situation in which my hands were shaking while I was holding the microphone.

Even after many years of experience, every once in a while, I do end up in a situation in which I get worried about the results and about what people will think. This usually happens when I leave my comfort zone and I am moving forward, taking a new challenge.

Yes, stage fright can have different forms of expressing itself and it could affect anybody, mildly or severely damaging their presentation. It is well known that very famous and successful performers suffer from stage fright. Some of them are Adele, Katy Perry, Rihanna and Lorde.

Of course, you could tell me they do not suffer from stage fright because they look great on stage! Actually, in these cases, they get nervous, but their bodies set off the fear alarm. They move forward and they go on stage anyway. Once you have accepted so many responsibilities, it is too late to walk away!

Stage fright does not necessarily mean you will have a heart attack if you step on a stage. Stage fright could be the nervousness and the worry that makes you drift away from connecting with your audience while, in order to protect you, your mind is scanning around for everything that is going wrong or that might go wrong.

When we are presenting ourselves in front of an audience, many eye balls are scrutinizing us. We feel exposed, or even naked. We leave the safety of being part of a crowd in order to lead the moment. People will listen to every word we say, so we better sound good!

When we leave our comfort zone, fear is activated as an alarm to protect us. Its goal is to make sure we will survive. If we listened to our fear every time we experience it, then some of the most relevant and amazing experiences in our lives probably would not have taken place.

Learning to ride a bike, attending a new school for the first time, deciding to move to a different city or following our dreams would not have happened if we had listened to that *fear alarm*. We would have canceled our plans in order to stay in the safety of the known territory.

Many actors say they are looking for roles that somehow scare them. That challenge is what keeps them growing and expanding. Even if they are scared, they do it anyway. That is the definition of courage. Being courageous does not mean not experiencing fear. It means to not to stop because of fear. It means moving forward even when we are scared!

If you are scared of presenting yourself in public, and you are still reading this book, it means it is important to you that you overcome this challenge. Otherwise, right now you would be watching a movie or distracting yourself in some other manner instead of reading these words.

Get the FREE VIDEO TRAINING at

http://www.lornavocals.com/p/speakoutbonus

Therefore, you are aware of the importance of taking a step forward. You probably have been "in your head", way too worried about the results or the opinion of others. Maybe, you are comfortable talking about your work or performing privately, and you notice that your performance has an inferior quality every time you need to be in front of a bigger audience.

As a vocal teacher and a music student for decades, I am used to the idea that no one sings as well in front of their instructor as they do when they are at home. Honestly, I cannot think of a single case in which a student did better in a class than when he was practicing by himself. Every time you present yourself in front of others, you will have to add the pressure of their opinion and their conclusions about you.

However, their opinion is completely out of your control. Chances are there is always someone out there who will criticize you. Also, there is always the possibility that you are going to make mistakes while you are being courageous enough to put yourself out there. This opens up the opportunity for other people to notice your flaws.

How to deal with fear

Practicing your courage will ultimately take care of your fear once your mind understands that you will not die after the presentation, even if it ends up being a disaster!

I once had a vocal teacher who said: "You need to suck in order to get better". There is no short cut. During my experience as a performer and coach, I could see very few people who had the opportunity of starting out by being gracious and not making mistakes at the beginning. Most of us, human beings, need to learn in order to develop and overcome every challenge. We need to have the courage to leave our comfort zone and accept that we are scared. We need to recognize it and, after analyzing the importance and the consequences of taking the chances, move forward anyway.

Get the FREE VIDEO TRAINING at

http://www.lornavocals.com/p/speakoutbonus

The repetition of this exercise will calm our fears and little by little, our errors will diminish in number and severity. Once we realize that not being perfect is not as bad as we thought, chances are that we will be able to BE more present, and less in our heads.

Quit trying to be perfect

Perfectionism kills dreams! If you are a perfectionist, you are eternally committed to frustration and unhappiness. But you are not alone. Every once in a while, I have got caught in this trap too. I need to confess that this has always been one of my main struggles.

Many times I had beaten myself up because of small mistakes that nobody else could notice but me. In those occasions, the need to perform at my best got me paralyzed.

However, that is one of my big takeaways about social media – giving me the opportunity to overcome my perfectionism. YouTube and Facebook have provided me with the space to recreate myself and to try again. It has given me the opportunity to practice how to be on camera, and it has allowed me to be okay with imperfection. The need to update all of my channels constantly, plus hundreds of live webinars and live classes I have hosted since 2013, have taught me how to be less exigent so that I can put my stuff out there.

As an online entrepreneur, I need to be constantly doing live webcasts, even if I am not always at my best, or have a team of hairdressers or makeup artists ready to assist me 24/7.

Many times I had to go on air without make up or without having the time to dry my hair. Little by little, I started feeling okay with that. That would not stop me anymore. Many times, only after finishing recording would I notice something had gone wrong. It could be the mic sound not being perfect, my blurred make up or an outfit that didn't look good. In those cases, after putting so much effort in the recording, I did not want to delete everything and repeat, especially since many of these videos were live and I had no way to modify them, unless I was able to travel through time!

You will be able to find videos with many flaws all over my social media. Nevertheless, the content I have been sharing is something that I am proud of. I have always been careful about delivering value. That value is what makes it worth for people to stop and pay attention to what I am sharing.

I do not mean that you should not care at all about your looks or that you should not invest on good quality images. What I mean is that social media is the place for people to know more about who you are and what you are about, even when you do not have a big production helping you out.

Marketing studies and results achieved by some of the most successful online marketers, influencers and famous artists with millions of followers have proven that posts with pictures and videos without any special production usually convert better and make a bigger impact than those that have a huge investment on cameras, lighting, etc.

People tend to trust people who look natural and who they can relate to. Nevertheless, in order to balance your branding and also to prove that you have a certain structure, it is also important that you always include a certain percentage of very well produced media.

Having a professional portfolio with nice head shots and also creating high quality videos for your products or for your YouTube channel can be nicely balanced with some natural selfies that show some of your daily life. This will generate a stronger bond with your followers.

After years of creating digital products and working online, I have made great friends through the Internet and I have met beautiful people who are my followers. Even being on the other side of the world, they have supported me and they have brought joy to my life. This sometimes comes as

---

Get the FREE VIDEO TRAINING at

http://www.lornavocals.com/p/speakoutbonus

an email, or even a comment on a posted video. Sometimes, it is a testimonial of a client who bought one of my products.

The bottom line is that if I had stopped myself out of perfectionism, or if I had refused to release certain content because the circumstances were not ideal, I would have not helped people who needed to learn from me at that moment, and I would have hurt my business by losing the opportunity to connect with new prospects or to even close new deals.

My saddest, most disastrous – but most profitable – live webinar

In January 2015, I lost my best friend, my 13-year-old cat Little Star. I had brought her with me from Brazil and she had been my most faithful companion since the day she was born. While I was staying briefly at a house of a friend in Van Nuys, California, while changing apartments, she somehow disappeared. Apparently, she went out when someone forgot the backyard door open. I did everything I could to find her. I was going out with a flashlight at four in the morning calling her. I spent months searching online, in animal shelters, posting flyers, knocking on the neighbor's doors, installing infrared cameras all over the area and even contacting a pet detective. I was desperate and devastated. At that moment, I was also very active on social media and I got many sales of my online vocal programs.

I told my followers what was going on. Many times, I could not hold my tears while doing Facebook live or Periscope broadcasts while I was searching. If you ever had a pet that became an important part of your life, I am sure that you can empathize with the desperation I experienced. Many of my followers did so too. I received so many messages from people all around the world telling me they were praying for me and for my cat, so that she could come back home! Some sent me ideas and case studies of cats who showed up even after a long time. They were trying to cheer me up so that I did not give up and abandon the search.

Get the FREE VIDEO TRAINING at

http://www.lornavocals.com/p/speakoutbonus

I was a mess, but I was still showing up in my social media channels. My followers were there for me too. At the time, I was running two live webinars per month which were the most important sources of income for my business.

Even when I was barely capable of managing all my responsibilities and was sleep deprived because I was spending the nights looking for my kitty, I scheduled a live webinar that I would broadcast from the university where I was teaching and studying at the time. I had a couple of hundreds of people who signed up for the event.

I looked and sounded terrible. I prepared my gear. The problem was that because of my stress, I forgot to pay attention to a series of details. To start with, I forgot my ring light, which is essential for all of my videos! Therefore, my image during the webinar did not look professional at all, since I was only using the normal lights of one of the classrooms.

I started the broadcast and I opened by being extremely honest about the situation with my cat. It was a class about singing, probably about how to sing high notes. Nevertheless, I spent some time updating my followers about the search and apologizing in advance if I was not as happy and energetic as they were used to seeing me.

I started the live class and more problems came up. I did not know that the room had a system to turn off the lights automatically. There was probably a way to deactivate this system, but I did not know how to do it! The result was that, every 15 minutes, the lights would go off and everything went black, so I had to rush and turn the lights on again!

After around thirty minutes, someone from the university administration kicked me out of the room from where I was broadcasting, since I had forgotten to sign up and fill the required paperwork. At that time, I was running a webinar with more than 100 people watching.

Get the FREE VIDEO TRAINING at

http://www.lornavocals.com/p/speakoutbonus

While still broadcasting, I left the room carrying my computer and I disconnected the external camera. I explained what was going on and I finished the webinar in one of the halls of the building.

I was so embarrassed! I was overwhelmed and ashamed by my lack of professionalism. At the end of the live class, when it was the time to start selling my complete program, after teaching vocal technique for an hour (including the interruptions), I was even scared to speak and ask for the sale! I wanted to disappear!

Nevertheless, I continued. What happened next was simply unbelievable! This ended up being my best-selling webinar ever! I had never sold as many programs and made so much money in such a short period of time in my life!

While I was doing that disastrous webinar, I thought nobody would buy, because of my non-professional presentation and all the technical problems involved. I decided to move forward just to teach, because I was already committed to go until the end.

Maybe the people who were at that webinar felt sorry for me and somehow tried to make me feel better by signing up to my program. I will never know. The fact is that it was the worst webcast with the worst quality of image and lighting I have ever done in my life.

Everything looked terrible, however I was being completely transparent. That day, I experienced a deep connection with the participants of the online class. Once again, I got convinced about the importance and the power of being vulnerable and real in front of my audience.

The importance of preparation and study

While telling you that being vulnerable and quitting perfectionism is the best way to connect with your audience, I do not mean that you should not try hard to improve and provide high quality content, services or products.

Get the FREE VIDEO TRAINING at
http://www.lornavocals.com/p/speakoutbonus

Preparation is key so that you can gradually improve and gain confidence while presenting yourself. Therefore, the more you practice and grow your knowledge in the subject, the expected tendency is that you start relaxing and feel more in control of the situation. With the consistent repetition and the right guidance, you will master your presentations.

The main problem is that, many times, the learning process can be frustrating when you do not have a system that will support your growth. Maybe you do not really know how to approach this challenge or maybe you do not have the opportunity to practice. Sometimes, you might even get too critical about yourself (the way you look or the way you sound) and those negative emotions might throw you off making you uncomfortable and upset.

As a vocal coach, one of the most interesting exercises I have been practicing with my students is the consistent recording of their voices. After practicing the vocal technique exercises and warm-ups, I would use an audio software to record them. Afterwards, we would listen back to the recording. Ninety percent of the time, at this point, I got a negative reaction from them.

Students who seemed confident while recording would get disappointed or even embarrassed after the playback. They would notice all the flaws, and their frustration would be noticeable in their faces. I have even felt some of them would have rather run out of the room than sitting there listening to their own voices!

In the next chapter, I will explore why we usually think our voices sound different when recorded. Now, I would like to explore the psychological aspect of this matter.

After listening back, I asked my students: "tell me what you liked about the recording". Most of them would answer: "Nothing!". This was the answer I

Get the FREE VIDEO TRAINING at

http://www.lornavocals.com/p/speakoutbonus

would get most of the time, especially with people who were starting out their studies with me.

When we are surprised by listening to a voice that sounds so different from what we thought would sound like and when we have the opportunity of analyzing it more objectively, we tend to get overwhelmed and reject the whole thing. We focus only on the negative and that disempowers us completely. We lose sight of whatever positive aspect we should be holding on to.

When I feel that a student is stuck in this state of mind, I insist, trying to regain the balance. I ask him to find at least one thing that sounded good. I do not continue with the class until this person is capable of acknowledging himself.

Only after he mentions at least one positive quality (even if it is a small thing, as the clarity of the words or the expression in a small phrase), I ask him about what he would like to improve.

Of course, 90 per cent of the time, I get a huge list of mistakes. Overall timber, pitch, rhythm, etc. Many times, some of them are not even capable of identifying what is wrong. They just know it is not good, and they do not like it. The problem is that in that moment they believe that not only are their voices not good, but they feel THEY are not good.

This is not just a game of words. If you can observe your voice or the way you look on camera as a separate thing from yourself and as a production of yours in a certain moment of your life, you will consider this as a stage you are going through. This is not a constant quality of your being and you are not stuck with it, just as the stage of a toddler who can hardly express himself does not define his future as a public speaker!

On top of it, if you cannot identify exactly what the problem is, which means you are unable to define in words what is the challenge you need to overcome, you will never be able to improve. Therefore, if you do not like

---

Get the FREE VIDEO TRAINING at

http://www.lornavocals.com/p/speakoutbonus

your voice at all and you do not do anything about it, you will most likely be stagnated in that stage forever, just believing that your voice is ugly. Therefore, chances are, you will never feel completely confident doing presentations.

When working with my clients, my number one concern is to identify the challenge and work with the precision of a surgeon on it. The reason for this is that in my early years of taking singing lessons, I would feel the frustration of practicing and spending time and money with private instructors, while I was not seeing any improvement at all!

I did not understand what was wrong, and I was simply repeating the songs over and over, which ultimately would lead me to reinforce the wrong practices, as opposed to replace them with more productive techniques that would help me move forward.

As a coach, I became obsessed with helping my students to identify their challenges, while focusing specifically on exercises that would transform every issue.

As an example, this is, more or less, the way dialogues go in my studio after showing my students their recording:

Me: So? What do you think? What did you like about it?

Client: Nothing!

Me: Nothing? Come on! I'm sure there must be something good in here. Think harder! We will not continue with the class until you mention ONE positive thing about your recording.

(After I insisted for a while)

Client: The first phrase sounded good. The part at the beginning. It has a good vibe.

Me: Excellent! Now, tell me what was the thing that you didn't like.

Client: My voice sounded weird in the second part.

Get the FREE VIDEO TRAINING at

http://www.lornavocals.com/p/speakoutbonus

Me: You mean you noticed strain when you started to run out of breath and then your overall sound changed?

Client: Yeah, yeah. That's it.

Me: Great! I will tell you why this is happening, and then we will start working on exercises that will dramatically improve this issue. Is that okay?

Client: Sure! Sounds good.

Me: At the end of the recording, you sounded tired. This happened because you were not using your voice in a productive way, which means you were not using your breathing support. When you condition your body to use the breathing support, you will find it easier to speak for longer periods of time and you will be able to say longer sentences without running out of breath. Therefore, your voice will stop sounding tired, because your timber will stay consistent now that you are not creating strain while speaking.

Client: So this means that I am potentially capable of speaking for longer periods of time without sounding tired?

Me: Exactly! Let's start working on your breathing. In a couple of weeks, you will begin seeing the difference!

I just gave you an example of the correct mindset that will help you detach from your lack of self-confidence as a performer. First, you need to gain perspective of how you look and sound, then you need to analyze your strengths. Later, you will define your challenges and you will plan how to consistently work in order to overcome them.

Once you understand that the stage you currently are at does not define your capacity, you will be able to implement the improvements. This, along with practice, will help you gain confidence.

Following the process I just described, you are actually *improving* yourself. You are not just being positive and sugar coating the situation.

Get the FREE VIDEO TRAINING at

http://www.lornavocals.com/p/speakoutbonus

Once you have covered the technical part, you will be able to relax more. Then, it will be much easier for you to connect with your mission, so that your passion and your knowledge can flow freely.

The famous ballerina Paloma Herrera, who was the first dancer of the American Ballet for years used to say. "I love practicing and rehearsing as much as I can. The more I rehearse, the more I am capable of letting go and enjoying the moment of the presentation for the audience".

<u>In order to deliver powerful presentations, you need to prepare yourself and practice by identifying and overcoming the specific technical issues that might be holding you back.</u>

In the next chapters of this book, you will find practical answers on how to solve some of the most common mistakes. Nevertheless, this is what a vocal coach can assist you with! This is my passion and my most developed skill. At the end of this book, you will find ways in which we can work together (in person or long distance, if you are not in Los Angeles).

Exercise: How to practice for your presentations

1) Record your presentation on audio or video, according to your needs.
2) Listen or watch back.
3) Say at least ONE thing you liked about it. After reading this book, you will be able to identify the most accurate way to describe every aspect. Write it down.
4) Identify what you did not like about it. Try to use the most accurate words so that you can define what is the specific problem.
5) Once you have identified the issue, work on the specific exercises to solve it.

Get the FREE VIDEO TRAINING at

http://www.lornavocals.com/p/speakoutbonus

6)Track your progress and you will see a dramatic improvement! Keep your old recordings for future reference.

Connection is EVERYTHING

<u>In order to deliver a powerful presentation, you need to stay connected to your mission and to your audience in an active dialogue, whether on stage in a live event, while talking to the camera or even during meetings.</u>

Some actors prefer working in the theater rather than tv or movies because of the energy and the magic of standing in front of an audience.
If you have the opportunity to perform or present your work on stage, you will be able to perceive the energy of the public. When it comes to bigger theaters, you might not be able to see people's faces. Nevertheless, you will feel how they respond to you. In smaller setups, you might perceive your audience's expression and, in case you are not following a strict script, you will be able to make adjustments according to their reaction.
When you are on camera, this can be a challenge, and some people have a hard time recording video or broadcasting live on social media because they are not receiving that instant feedback you get when you are physically standing in the same room with your spectators.
In any case, the connection is essential and it can always happen, either from the stage or after recording videos, only when you take the focus out of yourself and you open up your heart to feel other people's presence. As romantic and not practical as it might sound, I cannot find better words to explain it.
One of my amazing music performance teachers at the university, Dr. Abraham Laboriel is one of the best bass players in the world, and he has been recognized with several awards for being the most recorded bass player since 1971. He has worked with Michael Jackson, Madonna, Christina

Aguilera, Al Jarreau, Lionel Richie, and has played in several Disney's soundtracks and in many other top productions. He would always say, "when it's time to practice, study. But always put your heart on it. Even if it's a technical exercise, pour your emotion and have fun. Otherwise, when you are performing, if you have practiced being on auto-pilot, that will come out too, because you have conditioned yourself to perform without feeling. Always, prepare yourself and study to get ready for when the opportunity knocks your door. Then, when you are on stage, forget about everything. Just communicate!". He would tell the students: "when you perform, you should always have fun. That is why this is called to PLAY music. You need to PLAY!".

I will never forget his advice, which can be applied to all kinds of performances and presentations. Laboriel is well known for his groove and musicality and for his accurate technique while recording in the studio. Usually, he can nail a whole song that he has never played before just in the first take, a skill that only a few musicians in the world are able to achieve with such degree of professionalism.

That focus and quality of performance can only be the result of the capacity to be present, to be in the moment. To connect with your inner mission and to communicate with your public without getting distracted with your inner talk or worrying about technical details.

I invite you to cover several aspects that can help you improve your presentations by working on technique exercises. My goal is that you not only deliver a powerful performance, but I also want you to have fun and enjoy it as an opportunity to fulfill your mission and enjoy your passion.

Get the FREE VIDEO TRAINING at

http://www.lornavocals.com/p/speakoutbonus

CHAPTER 2: YOUR VOICE

"A rich, correctly-used voice is the greatest physical factor of persuasiveness and power, often over-topping the effects of reason".
(Dale Carnagey, "The Art of Public Speaking")

In case you are not 100 percent satisfied with your voice, in this section, you will find my answers to the most common complaints and questions I get about voice. At the end of this chapter, you will find what I call my "5 steps to a powerful voice", along with a list of exercises and the instructions to access the exclusive training that I prepared for you online.

A) VOCAL TROUBLESHOOTING

DISCLOSURE: THE FOLLOWING ANSWERS ARE BASED ON THE ASSUMPTION OF A HEALTHY VOCAL PHONIC APPARATUS.

Only a physician can determine the presence of lesions in your vocal chords as the result of vocal abuse.

Why does my voice lack projection or sound weak?

Short answer:

Reason 1: You are not using your resonators properly.

Reason 2: You are not using your breathing support

Reason 3: You are shy and consciously or unconsciously afraid or nervous about speaking in public, so you're holding your voice back.

Reason 4: Any combination of the previous answers.

Detailed answer:

Reason 1:

Maybe you feel that your voice is too weak or too low. Maybe you need to scream so that people can hear you. If so, this doesn't necessarily mean that

---

Get the FREE VIDEO TRAINING at

http://www.lornavocals.com/p/speakoutbonus

your voice IS like that. It could just mean that YOU ARE USING IT in that way.

By now, you probably know that you need a powerful voice so that your message can be delivered more persuasively and so that you can influence your audience. This is important if your professional success relies on how your voice represents your work.

If you are a speaker, your voice should be projected with confidence and effortlessly for long periods of time, so that you can maintain your audience's attention.

Speaking with a "shy" voice might give others the impression that you are afraid or insecure about what you are saying. If you are a lawyer, you need a strong vocal presence to reinforce your arguments in a trial or during negotiations.

The list of reasons why voice projection is essential for those who make a living out of their voices goes on and on, and the bottom line is that a poorly projected speech usually sends out a message of lack of authority or confidence.

However, the quality of the projection of your voice does not necessarily have to do with your volume. If you need to scream out loud so that people can hear and understand what you are saying, even in a small room, you might not be projecting your voice properly.

I am sure that you know some people who have a rich well-projected voice. When they speak, even at a normal volume, it is like their voices fill up the ambient. They are not screaming, or even being too loud. On the other hand, I am sure that you also know somebody else (this might even be yourself) whose voice sounds like the opposite. It is thin and weak, maybe even infantile, never powerful and it disappears fast without reaching the ears of those who are further away from the person talking.

Get the FREE VIDEO TRAINING at
http://www.lornavocals.com/p/speakoutbonus

According to the dictionary, resonance is "the reinforcement or prolongation of sound by reflection from a surface or by the synchronous vibration of a neighboring object". Therefore, vocal resonance is the phenomenon through which your voice will be multiplied after traveling through space when its wave sounds finds the opportunity to vibrate on different materials.

If you speak inside an empty cave, you will experience the intense echo and the resonance of your voice. What happens, though, if you fill up the cavern with pillows and mattresses and repeat the same words? Chances are your voice will be muted! The objects will absorb the wave sounds not allowing them to keep on traveling through space and multiplying its components, the harmonics.

If your voice has a poor projection, it probably has to do with the fact that you are not using your resonating chambers to multiply and improve your sound before it reaches the space outside your body.

Ideally, to achieve optimal results, your voice placement should be balanced between your mask and your mouth resonance before it goes out to reverberate in the ambiance or before it is even amplified by a microphone.

Imagine you want to throw a party, and you would like to encourage people to dance. Let's suppose that you have never thrown a party before, so you are not sure about what kind of equipment you need. You only have your computer with an amazing playlist of fast-paced dance songs. Would you expect people to dance and engage only by listening to the sound coming out of your laptop's speakers? I am pretty sure you would not even think of trying that out!

Would this inability to create an impact in your audience (your guests) and make them dance, have to do with the quality of the computer, or with your good taste as a DJ to select the best tunes to cheer up the party? Certainly not!

Get the FREE VIDEO TRAINING at

http://www.lornavocals.com/p/speakoutbonus

By now, you are probably thinking that the answer to this imaginary problem is obvious. You need to figure out some good speakers and, along with the speakers, a CABLE to plug the speakers into your computer.

I am using this analogy to illustrate what happens with our voices. If we want to impact our listeners, we need a way to amplify our sound so that our message resonates with them. We need not only good things to say. It is crucial that we deliver with enough power to move the audience.

Here is when I share with you the good news! You do not have to buy any expensive speakers. You were born with your own integrated ones! These are called your RESONATORS and they work through a principle not too different from the system that would amplify the sound of your laptop.

Your computer would function as your larynx, the source that originates the primary sound but which does not have an empty space sufficiently big and optimized in order to create a powerful sound. Your speakers would be your resonators, the empty chambers where the wave sound is multiplied and amplified efficiently.

So, now what? Now, you need a cable to connect the laptop to your speakers or, better said, your larynx to your resonators!

This imaginary "cable" is where vocal technique comes in! vocal technique exercises will teach you how to conduct the sound waves to your resonators so that you can improve your projection, just like a cable would connect your laptop to speakers!

When your voice is originated in your larynx after the vibration of the vocal folds, a very low volume sound is created. After that, the wave sound travels through the vocal tract, which is the empty inner space in your body that stands between your mouth and the end of your throat. You can see the end of your vocal tract by opening your mouth and looking in the mirror. Once in the vocal tract, the wave sound will be altered by the articulators, so that you can pronounce different words by moving your tongue, some in-

---

Get the FREE VIDEO TRAINING at

http://www.lornavocals.com/p/speakoutbonus

ternal muscles, and jaw. This is the key moment that will define if the good resonance will be permitted or not.

The resonance will happen only in an EMPTY space, and the wave sound will only travel to the resonators when the vocal tract passage is NOT OBSTRUCTED. Even if resonance happens in your whole body after the vibration of the vocal folds, the main and most effective results are defined by the use of your head resonance chambers. These are, mostly, your sinuses and the empty spaces in your vocal tract.

SELF TEST:

Find a pitch that you would engage in a normal conversation. Not a high pitch or a low pitch. Say hello, as you would usually say it when you pick up the phone.

Now, using the same pitch and pinching your nose, say MOOOOOOON MOOOOON MOOON and try to feel where your voice is vibrating. Is it in your throat? Is it on your chest? Is it on your mask? Is your sound being blocked completely because you are pinching your nose?

Result: This exercise will show you how your resonance is happening. In case you do not feel the vibration in your mask (sinuses area and nose) at all, we need to improve your use of the resonators! It means that your voice is stuck in your throat or chest, or only being amplified by your oral resonance. If your sound stops completely when you pinch your nose, your resonance is way too nasal. A well balanced and resonating voice will combine the right amount of nasal and oral resonance. You can start exploring how to improve this aspect of your voice by practicing the resonators exercise I prepared for you in the following FREE ONLINE TRAINING:

TO PRACTICE THE RESONATORS EXERCISE, ACCESS http://www.lornavocals.com/p/speakoutbonus

---

Get the FREE VIDEO TRAINING at

http://www.lornavocals.com/p/speakoutbonus

Reason 2: Breathing

When I was a teenager, I lived with my mom in Buenos Aires, Argentina. In that place, we had a very nice big white tile bath tub. I remember that even the first time I entered the house, the bathroom design called my attention and I got super excited while picturing myself taking long relaxing baths in it.

Unfortunately, the first time I tried to give myself the present of an at-home spa session (with candles included and all), I opened the tap and I found out a frustrating reality. Coming out of this beautiful fancy golden faucet, there was a weak trickle of water. I opened up the tap completely, and still, no more water or a stronger jet would come out.

Even if the stream was extremely hot, filling up that big bath tube would have taken hours, and once completed, the water would have been practically cold.

Then I decided to try the shower. The same thing happened. A weak trickle came out, hardly giving me the shower I deserved!

Sometime after that, my mom called the plumber. He said, "there is no pressure in the pipes". The solution? Practically none, unless we were willing to spend a lot of money to change the whole pipe structure.

The result: No baths at the bath tub for me and plenty of weak dissatisfying shower jets for years.

Don't get me wrong! I do not mean to complain about that house. I am very grateful I lived in that place with my family for years. I was very happy there.

I am just illustrating what happens when you do not have enough PRESSURE in YOUR PIPES but you TRY to have a powerful voice!

Get the FREE VIDEO TRAINING at

http://www.lornavocals.com/p/speakoutbonus

The airflow that goes through the vocal folds should come with enough pressure to make them vibrate without effort and to allow the wave sounds produced after the folds vibration to travel to the resonators.

Once again, here comes the good news! You do not need to change your pipes or spend any money on equipment! You just need to implement the vocal technique and applying the proper BREATHING SUPPORT.

This means that after reading this book, you will understand how to create the proper air pressure to have a powerful voice that will help you project better without having to scream.

Breathing support techniques are nothing more than re-learning how to use your body and your respiratory system in a healthy way, which will help you sound better and also prevent any vocal disorders.

When you engage your breathing support, you will be utilizing your abdominal and/or rib-abdominal breathing. More details about how to do this can be found in the exercises included in this book and in the exclusive FREE online training I prepared for you!

SELF TEST:

Is your breathing supporting your voice?

Stand in front of the mirror. Look at your shoulders. Breath in deeply. Did you lift up your chest or your shoulders while breathing in? If so, it means that you just used your chest breathing and you did not engage the proper breathing support. Try it again. Now, try to not to lift up your chest or shoulders. If this is still a challenge for you, you are probably only using your chest breathing while speaking or singing. This means that your voice could be a lot more powerful and beautiful if you would start practicing the proper technique!

Get the FREE VIDEO TRAINING at

http://www.lornavocals.com/p/speakoutbonus

ACCESS www.lornavocals.com/p/speakoutbonus to learn the FREE exercises.

Reason 3: You're holding back your voice
Stage fright is a reality for many people. Recent studies estimate that as much as 75% of the population struggles with the fear of public speaking to a certain degree. That means some 238 million people feel nervous about talking to others!

Because I have been performing since I was very young (I had my first dance recital at 4 years-old and my first TV appearance at 9), I am quite used to being on stage. I have danced, sang, spoken, played instruments and gave interviews. I have even performed in theaters in front of thousands of people in a series of concerts playing my songs with a symphonic orchestra. I have done hundreds of webinars, recorded hundreds of videos and studied with world-renown teachers, coaches, and musicians.

After more than 30 years of experience on-stage and on-camera, a degree in journalism, another in songwriting (Bachelor of music), and a career as an international vocal coach and musician, sometimes stage fright could still be a challenge for me. Of course, it doesn't paralyze me. I know about it, I know how to deal with it and I help people do the same. Some performers even say that a certain anxiety before their presentations keeps their adrenaline levels up and works as an incentive to stay passionate and connected. How is that possible? How can the top performers of the world be even partially influenced by any degree of stage fright? Well, you can find many famous artists who are still challenged by this type of anxiety. Some of these examples are super famous actors like Academy Award winner Jennifer Lawrence and also singer-songwriters like Adele, Rihanna, Lorde and Beyonce.

Get the FREE VIDEO TRAINING at
http://www.lornavocals.com/p/speakoutbonus

Yep, even Beyonce! She told Giant Magazine about her 2004 Grammy Performance with Prince: "Walking into rehearsals, I was just so overwhelmed and nervous! I was so scared and in my shell during rehearsals!". Moreover, she explained that Prince actually had to tell her to "belt it out."

Can you believe that? Someone having to tell Beyonce to "belt it out"? If you are not familiar with this term, "belting" is a technique that implies a powerful projection of the high notes as opposed to a light resonance in the head voice.

Could you ever imagine Beyonce holding back her high notes? Well, as you can see, at the end of the day we are all humans. This is why we all need rehearsals and this is why there are directors and vocal coaches. Ultimately, this is why I am writing this book.

Many times, we hold our voices back as a way of protecting ourselves when we feel overwhelmed, examined or judged.

When is a situation overwhelming enough to encapsulating our voices and blocking their natural projection? That depends. For Beyonce, it could have been playing along with Prince, probably because of how much she admired and respected him. To Adele, maybe only when she performs in front of big audiences since she feels more comfortable singing in more cozy environments or even writing her music in solitude.

For a college student, on the other hand, having to present a paper in front of the class or answering a teacher's question might be enough to let the anxiety take over and weaken his voice.

Because most of the human beings are moved by the need for growth and progress, chances are that we tend to hold back when we are in front of a new challenging situation that makes us feel insecure, or in a usual setup that somehow activates an emotional response of fear and the need to protect ourselves and hold back.

Get the FREE VIDEO TRAINING at

http://www.lornavocals.com/p/speakoutbonus

Our voices can expose ourselves in an extremely high level. I understood this when I first started singing on stage. I already had experience playing instruments (I played jazz piano in bands and studied classical guitar for years) and dancing (I studied ballet, jazz dance, and Classical Oriental Dance). Certainly, when I had to stand up on stage just holding a microphone, I felt lost, exposed, naked. It took a while for me to get used to it. At the beginning of my career as a student, my voice was very low and thin. I was shy, almost wanting to hide my voice instead of showing it off, which is the whole idea of singing, right?

Your voice will also carry your emotions and will be affected directly by stress. I already felt that immensely.

My mother passed away suddenly when I was 25 years old. Being raised in Argentina, and after the tough divorce of my parents, I was very close to her. She meant the world to me, even if we had our differences and we used to have many arguments.

At the time of her death, I was already a professional singer and I had just moved to Brazil, where I was participating in one of the first vocal tv contests at SBT channel. I was doing extremely well in the show and some of the producers had told me I was one of the favorites. They said I had a big chance to win.

The day after my mom's funeral, I had to show up for a new round of competitions. I decided to attend anyway, even if I was a wreck. I thought that was what my mom would have wanted me to do, so I did it for her. I could not sing though. I felt choked, my voice was not coming out at all. I was swallowing my tears and doing a big effort not to cry the whole time while I was in the studio. How could I even sing being in that state? I really did not care at all about my career at that point.

That day, I got out of the competition. They told me that it was because I did not sing well, and a producer, later on, told me that it was also because

---

Get the FREE VIDEO TRAINING at

http://www.lornavocals.com/p/speakoutbonus

my Portuguese had a slight Spanish accent. They did not want a girl with an accent to win the competition and be part of the band that would tour all over Brazil.

After that contest, I could not sing for two years. My voice would not project, it would not resonate. It was stuck in my throat. I was grieving. It took a long time before I could start getting my vocal power back.

Why do we hold back our voices?

Nowadays, I am very happy with my voice and my resonance but, every once in a while, I still feel anxious before performing in certain situations. According to my experience as a performer and as a coach for more than 350 clients over the past 15 years, the first step to deal with this tension is taking note of what scenarios make us nervous. Once we are aware of what is affecting us, the next step is dealing with it as opposed to ignoring it or trying to fake it.

These are some common emotional or psychological causes why our voices lack projection

- *Repressed emotions such as grief, shame or fear.* Like in my story when I was grieving for my mom, sometimes we hold back because we are not allowed to pour out all that we are feeling inside.

- *Fear of being judged or rejected by the audience.* We all want to be loved and accepted. When our focus is not on the connection with our message, we are scared that rejection will invalidate our speech or singing, and we give others the power to decide what is our worth.

- *Not feeling good enough, even after being prepared.* Sometimes, we have very high standards, and even if we practice and prepare, we still feel we are not good enough, or as good as other people we admire.

Get the FREE VIDEO TRAINING at

http://www.lornavocals.com/p/speakoutbonus

- *Not being prepared enough.* When you did not have the chance or the time to prepare your presentation, and you did not rehearse enough to feel confident.

- *Not knowing what you are doing.* When you did not have the education or support of teachers, coaches or directors. As an example, let's say that you do not like the sound of your voice but you do not know exactly why and you suddenly have to give a speech for the first time.

- *Competition or presentations that may define your future.* Thinking ahead about the consequences of your presentation, participating of competitions, or even the need to convince a jury or a business decision maker might be overwhelming if you are not well prepared to deal with such pressure.

- *Feeling intimidated by someone specific in the audience.* The presence of someone that we really care about might intimidate us like in the Beyonce's example I gave earlier in this chapter when she got nervous around Prince.

Why does your voice get tired or you even lose it after speaking?

Because of vocal abuse and strain. Poor vocal technique combined with an excessive demand for a certain period of time ends up disrupting the normal function of the vocal folds. In this case, these negative effects are not associated with other physical circumstances such as infections or cysts and might vary from a light hoarseness or vocal fatigue to a complete dysphonia. Continuous abuse and repeated episodes of dysphonia might be a sign of a more permanent vocal disorder or lesion, which can be diagnosed through an exam called stroboscopy, performed by your ear, nose and throat doctor.

Using your voice is a physical act that starts when you intend to talk or speak. Without thinking about it, you breathe out and the airflow goes through your vocal folds, which are located in the larynx, right behind where males have their Adam's apple in the front part of the neck. Every time you produce a vowel or a voiced consonant (like m, z or v, as opposed to voiceless consonants such as s and f) your vocal folds, which were until then resting at the sides of the larynx, move towards the center of the pipe and vibrate rhythmically when the air goes through them.

In case they are healthy and functioning properly, they will easily vibrate at different frequencies according to the pitch of the sound you are producing. Higher pitched sounds involve a faster vibration frequency in addition to a more extensive stretching of the vocal folds.

Now, think of your vocal folds as the branches of a tree that are moving when the wind passes through them. Imagine you love that sound. One night, there are strong winds that make the branches move violently and fast, generating a high pitched and loud volume sound.

Next, imagine that another day, you would like to reproduce that high pitch, loud volume sound of the branches moving fast. The only problem is that, on this specific day, there is no wind! Then, you try to climb up the tree and start desperately shaking the branches. You get tired, the sound can barely be heard and is not constant or consistent at all. You end up hurting yourself and you finally give up.

What I just explained, is an analogy of what happens when you are not using your voice properly and, nevertheless, you keep asking a lot of your vocal folds!

Your brain sends out an urgent message: a speech needs to be delivered or high notes need to be sung. However, there is not enough air pressure in order to make the vocal folds vibrate: the same that would happen when there is not enough wind to make the branches of a tree whistle.

In that case, your body compensation system gets activated. This is a mechanism through which certain structures end up assuming functions that should be performed by other parts of the body. If you cannot move one of your arms, the other arm will develop and compensate for the one that

---

Get the FREE VIDEO TRAINING at

http://www.lornavocals.com/p/speakoutbonus

is not functioning. If one ovary is removed or diminished in function, there is a tendency for the other to overdevelop.

If you need to lift up a very heavy object and you do not engage your core abdominal muscles and thighs, you might end up hurting your back. Your posterior thoracic muscles will compensate for the lack of strength of the tissue structures that should have been activated while performing a healthy and safe movement.

When you ask your voice to sing a high note and you do not provide the right air and amount of pressure by engaging your breathing support, other muscles in your larynx will try to take over and compensate so that the vocal folds vibrate and stretch, until you get the pitch and the duration you asked for.

Unfortunately, there is a price for this compensation. Ultimately it constitutes what we call vocal abuse. Soon enough, after a certain period of time that could vary from seconds to hours, your larynx muscles will give up and there will be irritation and inflammation. After that, the vocal folds lose their tonicity and their ability to vibrate rhythmically. They will not close completely anymore during phonation.

If you keep subjecting your body to this type of stress and abuse, you may develop a vocal disorder.

How can you avoid losing your voice and how can improve your vocal technique to prevent this problem?

You need to teach your body to perform the movements needed in order to have a healthy phonation, and you need to work out your breathing support so that there is no need to compensate by forcing the delicate tissues of the larynx. The proper vocal technique exercises will help you get prepared to use your voice for hours in a healthy way so that you can prevent hoarseness.

Get the FREE VIDEO TRAINING at

http://www.lornavocals.com/p/speakoutbonus

Quiz:

Do you usually get hoarse after speaking?

( ) always
( ) when I speak for more than two hours
( ) when I speak for more than one hour
( ) when I speak for more than half an hour
( ) if I scream too much at a sports game or concert
( ) very rarely

IMPORTANT: Losing your voice after speaking for an hour is not normal! It is a sign that you need to improve your vocal technique!

If you need to use your voice for several hours, it is imperative that you practice the exercises that will help you have a powerful and energetic voice.

Why does your voice sound weird or even different when recorded?

Short answer: when we speak, we listen to our voices from inside our heads. When we listen to a recording of our voices, we listen to what other people who surround us hear being outside of our heads, plus the specific technical influence of the device used to capture the recording, such as microphones of different qualities, cellphones, landline phones, webcams, radio transmitters etc.

In my experience, when I work with thought leaders who are starting to speak or record videos, I usually get the same answer when I ask them how they feel about their voices.

"I don't like my voice, please don't make me hear the recording," some of them say. "I hate my voice, I sound like a kid" or " I sound boring". Or "OMG, is that how I sound?".

Get the FREE VIDEO TRAINING at

http://www.lornavocals.com/p/speakoutbonus

Many people think they have an ugly voice just because they are not used to listening to their own voices and suddenly, after hearing themselves back, they get surprised or even disgusted.

Have you ever recorded a message on your phone and after listening back, you could not even recognize your own voice? Maybe you are one of those who has recorded their voicemail greeting a hundred times to erase it and re-do it, until finally giving up and getting to the conclusion that there is nothing to do about it. They are convinced that they have an awful voice. They end up setting the standard pre-set welcome message.

Then, these frustrated speakers tend to start criticizing their voices, trying to use several different disqualifying adjectives to describe their sound, or even feeling embarrassed because of it.

Honestly, even if not everybody has a pleasant perfect voice, I believe that 50 percent of the problem of people not liking the way they sound has to do with self-awareness and self-acceptance.

If you think that your voice sounds a certain way and, suddenly, when you hear yourself back you get a different result, 90 percent of the times this is not a pleasant surprise. The reason for this is that we all tend to be too hard on ourselves.

I have seen this dozens of times when I record my clients during our private vocal coaching sessions. However, I have noticed that after creating the habit of recording my students once a week, they start getting used to the sound of their voices. Then, they are able to recognize their strong points and their flaws without so much drama, even without taking it personally when there is something to be improved, such as pitch or even timber issues.

On the other hand, you should also consider what is the method you are employing to record your voice since the results will be influenced greatly because of this technical peculiarity. If you leave a message on a friend's

---

Get the FREE VIDEO TRAINING at

http://www.lornavocals.com/p/speakoutbonus

voicemail after calling him from your phone, and you listen back to the recording you just left, you are most probably going to be disappointed. Your voice will sound nasal, with a lot of treble and very few high frequencies or deep harmonics.

However, in case you record yourself with an iPhone using a memo recording app and you play it back, you will notice a difference between how the voice you just recorded sounds compared to your tone in the previous take on your friend's voicemail.

If you ever have the chance to record your voice with a professional microphone, like those used in big recording setups, you will notice that by using top quality equipment your voice will sound ten thousand times better. The reason for this is that those high-end microphones can cost dozens of thousands of dollars. They are the result of many years of research on how to make the artists sound better.

I would like you to consider that the sound of your recorded voice will be influenced by your microphone. Therefore, if you want to have a more realistic idea of how you sound or if you want to present yourself in front of your audience, you should consider investing in a good quality microphone for your recordings or live events.

Nowadays, with all the current technological advances, you can get a decent microphone at a relatively low price. You don't need to buy the most expensive one.

Why do I have an ugly, weird or not pleasant voice (or any other negative description about your own sound),and how can I fix that?

Short answer:

You are probably not used to hearing your own voice. In case you are actually used to hearing it and still think it is ugly, you can improve your overall sound by practicing the proper vocal technique.

Get the FREE VIDEO TRAINING at

http://www.lornavocals.com/p/speakoutbonus

Detailed answer:

"We need to work on your timber. You need to sound more like a woman. You sound like a child", my vocal teacher said after I finished singing a romantic ballad during our singing lesson. I didn't know what to say, I was embarrassed. I was frustrated. Especially, because I wasn't a kid. I was 22 years-old.

I always wanted to sing and I had found the right teacher. I knew she was trying to help me and not to discourage me. Nevertheless, I went home defeated. I don't remember anything that she said after that "child" sentence. After hearing that, I probably zoomed out and I just dived in the negative feeling of "not being good enough".

I am pretty sure that after saying that I sounded like "a child", she provided solutions and a positive approach in order to help me sound better. However, I was not able to listen to any constructive criticism. Don't we, not fully enlightened humans, tend to do that all the time when we feel attacked?

As an eternal student and instructor, I have noticed that one of the biggest challenges during the learning process is our "identification with the object of our art".

By saying this, I am referring to the fact that we usually take criticism personally, as if others were judging "us" as opposed to making observations about the product of our craft in a determined stage. Therefore, if someone would say to me: you sound like "a child", my immature mind (way over-identified with my voice as the representation of my value) would feel crashed.

The logical thinking process goes something like this: "I sound like a child, therefore, I suck…therefore, I am not good enough to be a singer… therefore I will never make it".

Do you get the idea? It is a circular destructive thinking pattern that does not leave any room to grow or to improvement, coming from the fallacy

Get the FREE VIDEO TRAINING at

http://www.lornavocals.com/p/speakoutbonus

that if some prodigies were born perfect, we all should be perfect since day one in order to be good enough.

After that devastating comment at my singing class that I still remember vividly after almost 20 years, I kept on going. I continued with my singing lessons and I followed all of my vocal coach's advise.

After months of hard work, I started noticing a change. I was singing challenging songs and my voice was not sounding childish anymore. Somehow, I started sounding like a sexy jazz singer! Who would have thought that I could ever reach that milestone? Thank God I was able to put aside my wounded ego after receiving some criticism! Thank God I kept going!

Most of us are way too identified with our voices as an extension of ourselves. We believe that the tone of our voice is an unmodifiable quality that we were born and stuck with for life, just like our height or the color of our eyes!

However, after more than 20 years of experimenting with my voice and more than 15 years of teaching vocals, I came to a different conclusion. Your voice and the way it sounds today is the result of the combination of different factors: physical, cultural and psychological, plus your specific vocal technique, which means how you are using your phonatory apparel.

I can easily prove this to you. Would your voice not sound different if you would have been born in a different country, speaking a different language Will your voice change or not during your whole life, since you were a toddler until you become an old person?

Your timber is the specific characteristic of your voice that allows people to recognize you when they are listening to you even if they cannot see you. Your timber will change with time and according to the way you use your voice.

Get the FREE VIDEO TRAINING at

http://www.lornavocals.com/p/speakoutbonus

If you still do not believe me and you think that your voice is not pleasant and that it will never sound better than it sounds today, just think about voice imitations.

Haven't you seen comedians imitating the different voices of ten, 20 or even 30 different people? How would that be possible if our voice was something that we are humanly incapable of changing?

The answer is that these imitators have developed a detailed analysis of how other people use their voices, and then, by reproducing these effects, they are able to come very close to the original.

They have a great capacity to hear how the resonators and the articulators are used in each case, and they study the typical sounds and personal style of every one of the characters they re-create. They might not be perfect, not sounding exactly as the original, but you must agree with me that they come unbelievably close and that they would fool many people if they would try to take the place of the original!

By using the example of the voice imitators, and my own example as a singing student, I am willing to demonstrate to you that you can actually choose how to use your voice in order to get better results.

In case your phonatory apparel is healthy, you can decide among a vast number of possibilities on how to utilize your voice. Every option will deliver a different sound.

Let's try something really quick… Say the word "hello!" as you would say it normally. Now, say, "hello!" while pinching your nose. Now say "hello!" imitating Mickey Mouse.

Were you able to make three different types of "hello!"? Well, there you go! That is the proof. Besides these three, you have an enormous amount of sounds that you could explore, only by modifying the position of your articulators and your placement.

Get the FREE VIDEO TRAINING at

http://www.lornavocals.com/p/speakoutbonus

Usually, we end up using our voice by default. What I mean by this is, most of us just talk without even thinking about how we are using our phonatory apparel.

We learn to speak by imitation of the people that surrounds us during our early years and we just go on with that. Many times, the fact that we have bad vocal habits is just the result of a non-ideal vocal model, which is the prototype of usage of the voice that we end up learning when we develop our ability to communicate verbally.

If people in your family speak loud, chances are that you will speak loud too. If they are mostly quiet and shy, you will probably follow that model. If your friends in school used a specific slang or a unique way to talk, you will be definitely influenced by them.

Along with these external features that are easily recognizable for everybody, you have also learned how to breathe, how to use your articulators and how to place the resonance of your voice. Of course, you have also integrated other people's gestures and other ways of non-verbal communication.

What I propose with my method of vocal technique is that you discover what the real possibilities of your voice are and what your best possible voice would sound like. This is the best version of yourself! I am not promising that you will change in one day by miracle and that suddenly you will acquire the timber of Louis Armstrong or Celine Dion. What I am inviting you to do is to learn how your body works and how to use it in the most productive way, so that you can get the best results possible!

Let me give you another example. If you are overweight, unless this is the result of some diagnosed disease, that overweight is most likely the visible consequence of your habits. These are the results of your diet and exercise routine. If you decide to change that, you will be able to discover a different

---

Get the FREE VIDEO TRAINING at

http://www.lornavocals.com/p/speakoutbonus

version of you, you will start looking better in certain clothes and, therefore, you will change your overall image.

The same thing happens with your voice! Once you learn how it works, how to use it correctly and once you start exploring its possibilities as a habit, you will be able to create an improved version of it, once you will have a large number of new possibilities that will be revealed to you!

Let me give you some examples of some of the most usual reasons why voices usually have certain negative attributes. In this table, I have included some of the most common complaints about how our own voices sound.

Non-pleasant vocal attribute	Possible Cause	Recommended Solution
Nasal Voice	Excessive nasal resonance. Once any physical disorder has been discarded by a physician, an obstructed vocal tract might be the main cause: low soft palate, and high tongue base.	Opening of the vocal tract. Practice of a more balanced placement: oral-nasal-mask.
Child's voice	Diminished space in the vocal tract. A small space caused by poor articulation stimulates the multiplication of higher frequencies that recreate a kid's voice.	Opening the vocal tract (soft palate, tong base, jaw, vertical articulation) to permit a deeper space and create more low frequencies that will balance the high ones. Mask full resonance.
Monotone voice (speaking with no pitch variations)	Pitch variations never explored. Vocal Folds never stretched out. Poor breathing support and resonance.	Vocal Folds Stretching. Breathing exercises, placement exercises. Slides, scales.
Low voice	Lack of resonance (projection), breathing and articulation. Vocal model learned in the early years. Personality trait.	Breathing, resonators exercises, articulators exercises

"Boring" voice	Monotone voice. Lack of expression and emotional connection with the words. Repressed emotions. Vocal model learned in the early years. Lack of rhythm and poor combination of speed and silence. Lack of expression in non-verbal communication and gestures.	Pitch exercises, gestures exercises, connection with the words, your mission and your audience. Including body expression: hands, facial and spacial on stage. Practice of pauses and enhancing words.
Overall "ugly" or "annoying" voice	When one of my clients say the word "annoying", most of the times, they are criticizing the sound of their recorded voice, since they can not clearly describe what is the negative attribute they are referring to.	*Detailed answer on "Why does my voice sound so different?"
Non-authoritative voice	Lack of connection with ourselves and our mission. Negative self-talk. Child's voice and low voice might influence. Poor support by non-verbal communication.	Connection with the mission, repeated practice in front of the mirror including gestures, hand movements, facial expressions and spacial use of the stage. Posture.
Airy voice	Air scape during phonation. Vocal folds are not closing perfectly and therefore, leaving an air escape. Possible vocal disorder or polyps. Some voices have a normal opening in the vocal folds that is not indicative of any vocal disorder.	After a medical exam, a professional will provide orientation on how to diminish the air escape. Improving breathing support and strengthening the vocal folds will give the option of a voice with more "edge" and "presence" and less "air".

Get the FREE VIDEO TRAINING at

http://www.lornavocals.com/p/speakoutbonus

Non-energetic voice	Lack of breathing support and resonance and poor articulation. Non-effective projection intention and/or mindset.	Vocal routines to strengthen breathing support and vocal folds. Mask resonance.
Tired Voice	Lack of breathing support and resonance and poor articulation.	Vocal routines to strengthen breathing support and vocal folds. Mask resonance.
Hoarse Voice	Possible damage by smoke, reflux or vocal disorders should be determined by a physician. If vocal disorders are discarded by a doctor, it could be lack of breathing support, resonance and poor articulation.	Ear, nose and throat doctor will determine the treatment in case of a vocal disorder or reflux presence. Once vocal disorders or other physical damage of the vocal chords are treated, a proper vocal technique routine will diminish functional hoarseness.
Shaky voice	Lack of breathing support and resonance. Nervousness	Vocal routines to strengthen breathing support and vocal folds. Mask resonance.

Get the FREE VIDEO TRAINING at
http://www.lornavocals.com/p/speakoutbonus

Why people ask me to repeat what I just said?

If people are asking you to repeat what you just said, they probably could not hear you, or they did not understand what you just said.

Of course, let's assume their capacity for hearing is normal and that, in case of speaking in a large room, you are using a standard microphone to amplify your voice.

Here are some possible causes why people are asking you to repeat what you just said.

- *You are not opening your mouth.* As obvious as it may seem, this is the main reason for a poor articulation and what causes people to not identify the words you are saying. If you do not open your mouth sufficiently, your sound will remain trapped in your vocal tract and you will not have space to pronounce correctly.

- *You are not articulating the words correctly.* You need to take the time to define every vowel and consonant so that every word is produced clearly.

- *You are speaking too fast.* It is crucial that you give yourself time to articulate every word, and it is also important that you give your audience time to process every idea you say. Make sure you are using pauses and that you maintain a rhythm that, without becoming way too slow, will allow others to absorb what you just said.

- *You have a thick accent.* Nothing against accents, okay? I speak three languages and I can assure you I still have traces of all of them every time I speak in any of them! Nevertheless, if your accent is too thick, some words might end up being confused with other words. In those cases, people may ask you to repeat what you just said. If this is the case (and this has already happened to me, so I can speak from my experience), try not to speak too fast and make sure to articulate the words properly. You can diminish your accent by taking lessons for accent reduction or even studying by yourself. I highly recommend the book "Mastering the American Accent". by Lisa Mojsin, in case you want to improve your American English.

-You are speaking at a very low volume. This might be caused by lack of projection, breathing support or even shyness. For more details, please refer to the section about "lack of projection" in this chapter.

-Your voice is not coming out because your pitch is way too low. I am not talking about volume, but about the pitch of your sound. Some people use their voices on an extremely low register that is not natural to them. Some of them try to make their voices sound more masculine or deep because they feel that their natural pitch is too high. This habit ends up wearing up the vocal folds and keep voices stuck within their chest resonance. Therefore, they can hardly be projected. The secret to a full deep voice is not speaking in a low pitch with chest resonance, but finding the sweet resonance spot for your voice and improving your placement and articulation, so that you can create more harmonics that will allow a rich tone and will balance any exaggerated high frequency.

Why do I sound boring? How can I fix it?

Short answer:

You can add "colors" to your voice by visiting different pitches, creating emotional momentum for specific words, playing with the rhythm of your phrases and taking advantage of the power of the pause.

Detailed answer:

First of all, please review the answer to the question: "Why does my voice sound different when recorded?" I am asking you to do this because it is very common that people who are not used to listening to their own voices get a negative impression when they listen back to themselves. A 'boring" voice is a very common observation they make in those cases, and it has to do with how surprising it gets when they realize they were not as energetic as they thought they were while speaking.

The bottom line is that we need to be extremely enthusiastic/energetic when we are recording and that most of the times this can feel a little over the top if you have more of a mellow or discrete personality.

Have you ever heard that statement that says when you are on camera you look about ten pounds heavier than you actually are? They said that is the reason why models and actors usually look so much skinnier in person! Well, something like that could be applied when it comes to the energy of your recordings or when you are on stage. If you are making a podcast or a video, or if you are performing at a live event, you will need to add some extra energy (I would say at least 30 percent) so that you can keep the energy levels up and you do not lose the attention of your audience.

And how to do that? You do not need to scream! Enhancing your voice and projection through vocal technique, including hand movements, facial expressions and improving your body language will help you keep the momentum going.

In addition, it is very important that you utilize different pitches during your talk, visiting highs and lows and creating an interesting melody to avoid a monotone voice.

You should also play around with the rhythm of the words you say and with the performance of every word according to their significance in order to keep your audience's interest.

Why do I sound like a kid?

You might think so after listening back to yourself if you are not used to it, so let's contemplate the possibility that you might be getting the wrong impression because of the surprise. If you are still positive that you sound like a "kid", you might need to improve your timber by adding low frequencies that will create a deeper voice. You can achieve these results through articulators, breathing and resonators exercises.

If you came up with the idea that you sound like a child after listening to your recorded voice, please refer to the answer to the question "Why does my recorded voice sound so different" in this chapter. If somebody else gave you some feedback that confirms this suspicion, do not worry, we can still work it out! I have done this myself, with my own voice and I have confirmed it by helping dozens of my students around the world.

The reason why certain voices sound "infantile" or like "kids" has to do with the use of the articulators and the resonators.

High frequencies, which are the characteristic frequencies of children's voices, will multiply in small spaces, while low frequencies (characteristic of "grown-ups" and males) tend to intensify in wider spaces.

If you are not opening the space of your vocal tract and if you leave just a very small empty space inside your mouth, there will be a tendency to multiply the higher frequencies, and your voice will sound mostly high-pitched and thin. These kinds of sound waves tend to reverberate towards the upper part of the head, making the sound even more metallic.

You need to create a deeper space inside your mouth to allow the wider sound waves to dissipate and you need to learn to place your voice in your mask so that you achieve a fuller and richer tone. Articulators and resonators exercises will help you reveal a more balanced voice sound.

I have an accent and that makes it harder to be a good speaker and singer. This is affecting my self-confidence. What can I do?

As you know by now, I am a trilingual voice coach. I was born in Argentina, but my father's family is British, so they usually talked to me in English when I was a kid. Later on, I moved to Brazil and I started speaking Portuguese. Years later, when I relocated to Los Angeles, California, I felt the

Get the FREE VIDEO TRAINING at

http://www.lornavocals.com/p/speakoutbonus

need to improve my English accent and I started trying way too hard to sound like an American.

What was the result? Most of the time people asked me if I was Russian! Nobody has ever guessed that I was born in Argentina! However, I will not pretend this is a minor issue for me or something that I completely overcame. While being a voice coach and singer-songwriter based in LA, for some time I beat myself up because of my accent and I did not take some opportunities to put my work out there because my accent made me feel insecure. I tried to hide it. I tried to avoid it big time!

Nevertheless, one day, at one of my songwriting classes with professor Michael Bradford while pursuing my Bachelor's Degree, I begin to see things quite differently. Bradford is a world renown musician, songwriter, and music producer. He has already produced albums for Madonna, Deep Purple, Steve Nicks and Anita Baker, among others.

During his class, he said: "You guys, coming from other countries, have something different, something exotic that makes you unique. That is your accent! You, singers, don't get rid of it! Embrace it!".

At first, that was hard to swallow, but it ended up making sense. After that day, I kept on working on improving my American Accent but I also made peace with the fact that I will never sound 100 percent American.

Of course, nowadays, in times when immigrants are not very welcome in the United States by some of the political authorities, and when there is an actual movement oriented to reject and make difficult the integration of people from other countries into the American society, this could be a challenge. Having an accent can make us feel like outsiders, even if we are trying hard to belong. Having an accent might make us feel insecure when we present ourselves on-camera and on-stage. The pressure is on, and while speaking we get worried about the way we pronounce the words. We are concerned about the right use of the tenses. Yes, "tenses"! We really get tense(s)! ;)

Something interesting happened to me some time after the advice given by my teacher about embracing the uniqueness of our accents. Months later, I posted on Facebook offering some free vocal coaching sessions to members of marketing and self-development groups that I am part of. The idea was having the opportunity to know more about the vocal needs of people from all over the world as part of my field study for the preparation of this book and for my new online training programs. Through these Facebook groups, I ended up meeting one-on-one with more than 50 people from all over the world.

To my surprise, this issue about the accent that I had been facing myself was more common than I thought. The people I coached for my study were authors, online entrepreneurs, coaches, and businessmen. Most of them spoke English as a second language and they were going through the same struggle I did every time they had to go on stage or on camera. Their accent made them nervous and was a distraction to them while they were speaking. Even though I am still working on my American accent, and I still have a lot to improve, I understood that my message is universal. I can translate it from one language to another, and that is what I actually end up doing every day! While teaching through Skype from my studio in Hollywood, I end up coaching in up to three languages on the same day. I might be talking in Portuguese with a Brazilian student who lives in Dubai, an hour later teaching in Spanish to a Mexican singer who comes to my studio, and later on, in the same day, I might be recording some vocal lessons in English for my YouTube channel.

The thing is that getting completely rid of an accent is very hard, especially if you are improvising. Fixing it for a song can be easier because you can repeat the take at the studio until you get the desired result.

Get the FREE VIDEO TRAINING at

http://www.lornavocals.com/p/speakoutbonus

I am not saying that you should not care about your accent or about speaking a second language as accurately as possible. What I mean is, even if you work hard at it, there will always be a little bit of an accent that will stick and remain. That is just who you are, your story and your roots that are still present.

Don't you think that this accent could be the proof that you have a more extensive background, which allows you to analyze your topic from different perspectives? Have you ever thought that there are many people out there who need your help as a professional, and who live outside the US, but who also speak English as a second language? They have an accent too! They get you!

If you have an accent, I would suggest that you keep on trying your best to reduce it as much as you can for a matter of clarity and to be able to express yourself in a professional and confident way. As I mentioned before, I recommend the book "Mastering the American Accent", by Lisa Mojsin. This edition even includes Audio CDs so that you can practice on your own.

Nevertheless, do not get too obsessed with this subject. Practice speaking and lecturing on your second language as much as you can, and be okay with the fact that you will always keep a touch of your charming accent as a souvenir from back home!

My voice is too loud or too harsh. Can I fix it?
In this case, you have probably developed a way of using your voice that does not leave space for nuances or subtle performances. In order to be a better speaker, it is crucial that you explore new forms of communicating different emotions and ideas so that you can keep your audience engaged for longer periods.

Get the FREE VIDEO TRAINING at

http://www.lornavocals.com/p/speakoutbonus

Vocal technique exercises will help you control the quality of your voice by understanding how to change the sound, pitch, volume, and timber. Once you comprehend what is the right amount of air pressure and the amount of air that you need to speak efficiently, you will be able to master the results of your overall sound.

Your body language and the performance of your voice will help you create a speech that better represents the message you are trying to convey.

I speak too fast (or too slow). Is that bad?

I have been guilty of this one too! For a long time, I felt like I was in a race, trying to make all the words I needed to say fit in whatever space of time I was given. I used to speak extremely fast, just like most of my friends. Endless phrases connected without a pause. One idea would be linked to another and there was not even a second for those who were listening to even comment on the topic that I was lecturing about!

Fortunately, some friends told me about this speaking trait of mine, and I started practicing a better-paced speech. I realized that my hurry had to do with some kind of uncertainty and insecurity. I had too much to say, while I did not know if my listeners would stay until the end to hear it all!

I also believe that I was explaining myself way too much, trying to expose new proof so that my audience would have a higher opinion of me and so that they would recognize me as an authority. Actually, with time, I realized this was not the best way to influence them.

Later on, I understood that less is more. A very well thought and low paced sentence is a lot more effective than an infinite line of phrases trying to make a case.

Keeping the right rhythm and giving yourself time to choose the right words, using pauses and commas to give your audience time to think about what you have just said, and even creating some suspense about what is to come will always work best. Therefore, a better-delivered speech will help you sound more confident.

On the other hand, when you engage your body to support the words you are saying and when you use gestures to illustrate the phrases, you will find that your speaking becomes much more effective and compelling. You will sound more confident and present, and then your speech will be more persuasive.

My voice is too nasal. What can I do?

If you think that your voice is too nasal, please make sure that trustworthy people confirm or deny this suspicion. In case everybody agrees that that is the case, by applying the correct vocal technique, you can improve this issue dramatically

First of all, you need to be aware that there are two main ways of amplifying your voice according to the placement of your resonance.

There is the nasal resonance (when the sound waves travel their way towards the sinuses and nasal cavities) and there is the oral resonance, towards your mouth, which will not provide a good amplified sound on its own but which needs to be included in order to obtain a well-balanced full resonating voice.

When the base of your tongue is too high and/or the soft palate stays down without opening up the space of the vocal tract, most of the air and the sound waves originated in the larynx end up being forwarded towards the nasal cavities. This creates an exaggerated nasal sound.

Therefore, in order to correct this matter, you need to learn to modify the position of your soft palate and the base of your tongue, so that you can control the nasality of the sound.

Get the FREE VIDEO TRAINING at

http://www.lornavocals.com/p/speakoutbonus

Speak out! 75

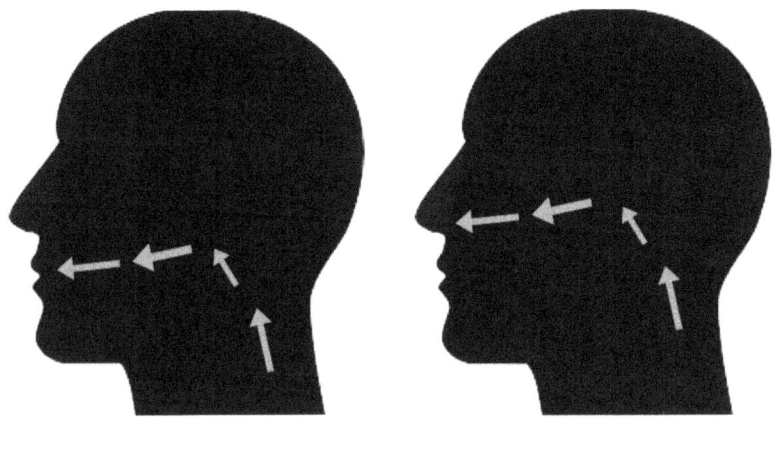

Oral Resonance   Nasal Resonance

SELF-TEST

In order to better understand your current vocal condition, take the following test. There are no right or wrong answers, and there are no grades, either!

Do you feel tight while you are speaking? Do you experience any pain in your neck or shoulders?

Yes
No

Do people usually ask you to repeat what you just said because they could not understand your words?

Yes
No

Get the FREE VIDEO TRAINING at

http://www.lornavocals.com/p/speakoutbonus

Do you like the sound of your voice after recording it?

Yes

No

Do you feel like your voice is powerful and projected easily?

Yes

No

Breathe deeply. Did you lift up your shoulders while breathing in?

Yes

No

Do your phrases fade away at the end as if you were lacking energy?

Yes

No

Is your voice monotone? (It seems like you are using always the same pitch, without variations)

Yes

Get the FREE VIDEO TRAINING at

http://www.lornavocals.com/p/speakoutbonus

No

Do you experience hoarseness after talking for an hour or less?

Yes
No

Pinch your nose gently and say aloud: "Oh, Oh, Oh." Do you feel any vibration in your fingers?

Yes
No

Does your voice sound too nasal, as if you were congested?

Yes
No

B) THE 5 STEPS TO A POWERFUL VOICE

Romaira Dias de Carvalho had been singing at church for years. Even so, she had always felt her voice was weak. Even when she desperately wanted to sing, she always thought that she did not have the talent to perform. However, in 2017 she found one of my free vocal lessons on YouTube and, later on, decided to sign up for one of my online complete programs. After just one week of training with my method, she posted the following message at my student's Facebook private group:

"I am so grateful! Yesterday at choir practice, I noticed a huge progress in my voice! We were all very tired, and I thought that because of this, singing would be nearly impossible for me. Nevertheless, I realized that, without even thinking about it, I was already applying what I learned with the vocal exercises I had been practicing with Lorna's program for the past week. The practice was already making a difference! My body started to respond automatically according to the new technique, even with an improved breathing. I got so impressed! Just a couple of weeks ago, I was getting dizzy while starting to sing, but this time that did not happen at all and by applying some of Lorna's simple tips (such as opening my mouth vertically) my voice came out a lot more freely! Every time I hit a high note, I was happily thinking of you, professor Lorna! Thank you".

Get the FREE VIDEO TRAINING at
http://www.lornavocals.com/p/speakoutbonus

My online student Romaira Dias de Carvalho

This testimonial is just one among dozens of similar cases. I get very happy every time I receive one of these, so if you want to let me know about the progress you have experienced after learning with me, please post it on my Facebook Page and leave a review! This is the link: https://www.facebook.com/lornaeofficial

In this case, Romaira confirmed once again the effectiveness of my 5 steps to a powerful voice® when it comes to the singing voice! However, this five steps work for both speaking and singing. Here is what they are about.

First, you need to understand the mechanism through which your body produces sound. Then, you will start practicing the vocal exercises that will introduce the right way to use your voice, so that your brain gradually gets used to it. After a little while, since this is the most efficient and healthiest option, you will start using the right technique without even thinking about it. The results will be noticeable.

Suddenly, you will start speaking with more ease, even in situations that would have been extremely challenging in the past. This works like magic!

If you have read the previous section of this chapter with the most common questions and vocal issues and its causes, you have already understood that, unless there is a vocal disorder, pretty much every vocal challenge that might be holding you back can be corrected through the practice of vocal technique.

After 15 years of experience coaching singers and speakers and also by being a singer and speaker myself, I have learned that the biggest frustration for vocalists consists of being capable of imagining the sound they want to create, and not knowing how to actually reproduce it with their bodies.

Even if you are not a singer, you know exactly what I mean! You could easily imagine a beautiful high note, but actually hitting it gracefully once you open your mouth ends up being a whole different story!

Our voices and our phonatory apparel are amazing perfect machines capable of producing an enormous amount of different sounds. These potential sounds will only be available to use if we actually know how to reveal them according to our capacity of exploring its different features.

Imagine that you get the most modern and expensive cellphone available in the market, but you are not familiar with technology. This cell phone seems to have only one main button in the front, and a couple of buttons on the side for volume control. Probably, in the beginning, you will only use the cell phone to receive and make phone calls. Little by little, you will start discovering the new possibilities of your device by downloading apps, taking pictures and even editing them! Gradually, you will learn about the hidden capacities of this marvelous invention!

The same thing happens with your voice. You can spend a lifetime using it intuitively and in a way that is the most natural to you unless you see yourself in a situation in which you will ask more out of it than just the minimum. That minimum will be enough for you to get by until the day you

---

Get the FREE VIDEO TRAINING at

http://www.lornavocals.com/p/speakoutbonus

need your voice to communicate more efficiently and to make a bigger impact in your audience.

Then, under pressure, the usual minimum will not be enough. You will need to take a step further and master your voice!

Let's imagine you have the opportunity to pitch a very important project in a business meeting, you need to train a group, or you were asked to lead a speaking event in which you will have to talk for hours. This is when you need to UPGRADE your voice!

Don't worry, this "upgrade" does not imply getting a brand new voice! It will only require that you learn how to use the one you already have more effectively so that you get the best results possible.

Professional speakers and business people who make a living out of their voices are nowadays forced to take better care of their vocal instrument. Two of the best paid personal development coaches and thought leaders in the world, Brendon Burchard and Tony Robbins, have already made public that they needed the emergency help of a vocal coach after their voices were gone due to vocal abuse.

Burchard explained that once he had to look for a vocal coach in the last minute so that he could complete the three days of one of his sold-out live events. He got absolutely dysphonic after speaking for a whole day from the stage.

He said that after that episode he understood the importance of learning how to use his voice properly in order to fulfill his professional endeavors.

Speaking in a live event for eight hours is like running a marathon. A marathon will require a lot more from you than what a 30-minute run would. Would you sign up for a marathon without getting in shape first, acquiring the right gear and making sure you are applying the best possible technique in order to make it until the end without hurting yourself?

Probably not.

Get the FREE VIDEO TRAINING at

http://www.lornavocals.com/p/speakoutbonus

This is why in order to get the best out of our voices and get ready for bigger challenges, there is a formula we need to fulfill:

TECHNICAL CONDITIONING + PHYSICAL CONDITIONING

Technical Conditioning: You need to learn the most productive way to use your voice so you can get the best possible results. This implies learning how to breathe and how to use your resonators and articulators, among other things.

Physical Conditioning: You need to strengthen the muscles that are involved in the production of your voice. This includes your diaphragm and some of the articulators such as your tongue and lips.

This formula can be applied to a variety of physical activities. For example, if you are willing to lift up some heavyweights, first you need to understand the right way to perform every movement. By observing all the details, you will make sure that you are protecting your body so you do not get injured. Once you are comfortable with the repetition, the correct moves will become natural to you, and you will not even have to think about it. This is what we call technical conditioning.

Still using the same example, once you have mastered the technical part of this specific weightlifting, you will still need to strengthen the muscles of your arms in order to be capable of performing the movement that will elevate the weights. This is what we call the *Physical Conditioning*.

I have already taught vocal technique for eleven hours in a day (50 minutes of class per student). In these extreme cases, I felt tired afterwards, my body was exhausted. Nevertheless, my voice was intact. There was no trace of hoarseness. The reason for this is not that I am particularly talented.

Get the FREE VIDEO TRAINING at
http://www.lornavocals.com/p/speakoutbonus

This is just the result of years of constant physical and technical conditioning.

What are the benefits of learning vocal technique?

Mastering your breathing will have a direct impact on your emotional state during presentations. It will help you stay calm and in control, it will make your voice resonate and project strongly without you having to try too hard, and it will pace the rhythm of your performance. Mastering your vocal technique will help you feel more confident and prepared when you are facing your audience. After achieving your physical and technical conditioning, you will TRUST your voice and you will KNOW that this is one of your STRONGEST assets. You will have strengthened the skill that plays the main role in your presentation: the one that determines your efficiency to deliver your message.

The 5 steps

Step 1. Relaxation

Have you ever tried to talk and felt as though someone was choking you? Have you ever got so tense during a presentation that your voice started shaking and people got aware of how nervous you were? If so, you already know why relaxation is so important when you are counting on your voice to do your job!

Relaxation is essential for two reasons:

- *Psychologically*. If you are worried, nervous, angry or insecure, chances are your body will be affected. You can even suddenly lose your voice, feel your words and your hands shaking or get a dry mouth. I'm sure you can add a million more possible horrible scenarios that could ruin your performance and blow your chance to win your audience! This is why in the first chapter of this book we have approached the importance of your "connection" and

Get the FREE VIDEO TRAINING at
http://www.lornavocals.com/p/speakoutbonus

other mental and emotional issues that are crucial in order to get you ready to present yourself in public, even under pressure.

- *Physically.* The tension in the muscles of your shoulders, neck, and throat will tighten up the delicate structure of your larynx, obstructing the free movement of the vocal folds that stretch and shorten while vibrating as the airflow goes through them. Every time we say a syllable, the vocal folds that were resting on the sides of the voice box will close and adjust the pitch while being stretched by cartilages.

If you have tension on your shoulders, it will travel like electricity to your larynx, and this will create tightness in your vocal folds. Therefore, it is crucial that before every presentation, you go through a thorough relaxation sequence. This will clear the tension so that your voice comes out more freely. Imagine you are trying to open a door, but there is someone that is on the other side blocking the way. What would be easier? To keep fighting against the resistance of the person on the other side or to ask him to move so that you can open the door easily? Starting your presentation without having performed a relaxation sequence might make your work a lot harder than it should be.

Access here the free sequence of relaxation exercises:
http://www.lornavocals.com/p/speakoutbook

Step 2: Articulators

Once the primary wave sound originated by the vibration of the vocal folds has traveled upwards through the vocal tract, the original sound is transformed by the shape and the position of the articulators. Some of them have a fixed position, like your teeth and your hard palate, and other can be moved in order to modify the wave and create diverse words with different timbers.

Just like a violin has a specific shape that determines the quality of its sound, the shape formed by your articulators will change the tone of your voice. This will affect the manner the waves are amplified and will also provide an available repertoire for creation.

In order to have a powerful voice, you need to strengthen your tongue, lips, and inner cheeks, and you also need to be capable of adjusting the position of your soft palate. The more toned all these muscles are and the more control you have over them, the more clarity you will achieve to emphasize your words.

Check out the answer to the question on "I have a nasal voice. What can I do?", included in the previous chapter, to understand how your articulators can radically modify the overall sound of your voice.

Articulators exercise:

The goal of this exercise is to strengthen the muscles involved in your articulation and to gain clarity while pronouncing every word with ease.

- Grab a wooden stick or a clean pencil or pen.
- Put the wooden stick or pen between your upper and lower teeth, placing it right beside your canines.
- Without letting the stick or pen fall, read the page of a book while trying to speak with as much clarity as possible and moving your upper lip.
- Once you have finished reading the whole page, read the first paragraph without the stick or pen. You should be able to notice the results of this exercise and therefore speak with more ease than before!

Get the FREE VIDEO TRAINING at

http://www.lornavocals.com/p/speakoutbonus

Access the video demonstration to this exercise by accessing this free link http://www.lornavocals.com/p/speakoutbonus

Step 3: Breathing

Testimonial:

"Thanks so much for your time today. After just our first half an hour together, I'm breathing easier than I have had for nearly 3 years. I can see how not only will my voice be dramatically different in a fairly short time, but also the exercises you have given me have already stopped me feeling like I'm working hard just to get air into my system". (Shelley Holmes, speaker and author, Australia)

Breathing is the foundation of vocal technique! Nevertheless, you can only achieve an optimal breathing by making sure that the other four steps mentioned in this chapter are also being taken care of. Especially, you will not be able to breathe correctly if you are not relaxed!

I could write a whole book just on the topic of breathing, and it would easily fill out 100 pages! Breathing is a vital function, however most of us have never even stopped to think about it. We usually breathe by default and, unfortunately, nowadays that standard mode is not the healthiest or most productive when it comes to taking care of our voices.

Let's do a quick test together. You do not even need to put this book aside. Go in front of a mirror. Looking at yourself, simply breath in deeply and breath out. Did you lift up your shoulders while you were breathing in? If so, don't worry, you are like 95 percent of the students I have ever coached. The majority of the other 5 percent had already learned about breathing with former instructors!

If your chest and/or your shoulders went up while breathing in, it means that you are using your "chest breathing". This type of breathing is the same one that we use when we are afraid or agitated. When we are in emergency mode, shallow breathing and a fast heartbeat will get us ready for a faster response in case we are in danger. Not surprisingly, you might have experienced this in case you have ever suffered from stage fright!

This type of breathing is part of our automatic survival mode but is not beneficial when it comes to your vocals. In order to have a more powerful voice, you need to start by practicing your abdominal breathing instead of your chest breathing. Ideally, if you were being coached by me, after practicing your abdominal breathing for a couple of months, you would take a step forward and learn the rib abdominal breathing. The latter is the most advanced technique that will allow you to get the best out of your voice, especially if you want to become a professional speaker.

Chest Breathing: small amount of air inhaled and available for speaking and singing. Long phrases are not supported. No breathing support. You will need to inhale more frequently.

Abdominal Breathing: Larger amount of air inhaled, to almost full lung capacity. Medium or long phrases will be supported. Allows breathing support. Less frequent inhalations needed.

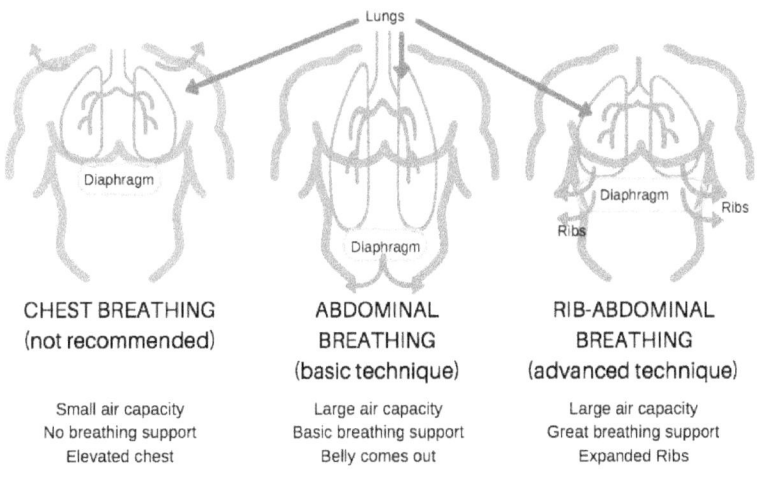

Get the FREE VIDEO TRAINING at
http://www.lornavocals.com/p/speakoutbonus

Rib Abdominal Breathing: Larger amount of air inhaled, to almost full lung capacity. Long phrases will be supported. Optimal Breathing support. Less frequent inhalations needed.

<u>In order to have a powerful voice, you need to condition yourself to use the abdominal breathing, the rib abdominal breathing, and the breathing support, while avoiding using the chest breathing.</u>

Abdominal Breathing Exercise:
In front of a mirror, put a hand on your belly (right beneath your belly button) and another on your chest.
Breath in trying to relax your shoulders so that you do not lift them up and do not elevate your chest.
Imagine the air is going right into your belly. Hold the air in for two seconds. Breath out.
If you are still lifting up your shoulders while breathing in, it means that you still need to practice more, but you will soon be able to make it! I promise! You can try this exercise while laying down on your back as well. This position might facilitate the motor coordination. Once you are able to keep your chest relaxed while breathing in and just letting your belly expand, you can try the exercise again while standing up.
During the abdominal breathing, you will feel like the air is going to your belly. That air is actually filling up your lungs and expanding into your abdomen while pushing your gut out.

Breathing support
Let's try out something else together! Breath in, and try to blow out the air you got inside by creating a constant airflow that lasts as much as you can.

Get the FREE VIDEO TRAINING at
http://www.lornavocals.com/p/speakoutbonus

How did it go? Were you able to create a perfect constant airflow until you blew out all the air? Or did you feel that the airflow faded away as you moved towards the end? Chances are, in case you have not practiced breathing exercises before, your airflow faded out.

Probably your airflow would look something like this:

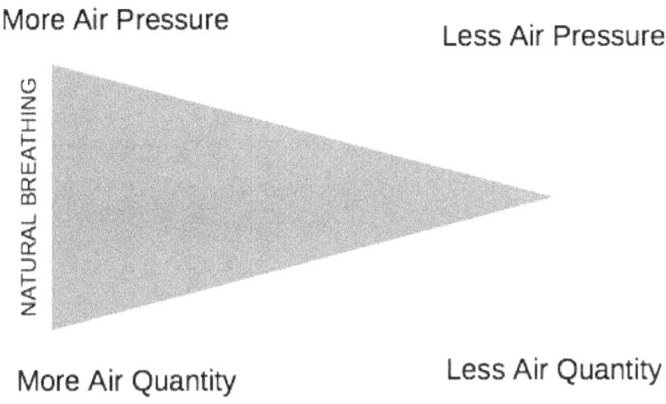

When we speak, we do not want our voices to fade away every time we get to the end of a phrase, right? We want the opposite! (By the way, if you have experienced your voice fading out or your pitch getting flat at the end of the phrases while singing, this is probably the main reason). The fading out of the exhalation is perfectly normal as part of the natural movement of your diaphragm.

However, in order to get the most productive results from our voices, we need to create a continuous airflow all the way until the end. Then, we will be able to start and finish sentences with an even pressure and without falling apart at the end of the phrases. This is why we need to utilize the "breathing support".

Get the FREE VIDEO TRAINING at

http://www.lornavocals.com/p/speakoutbonus

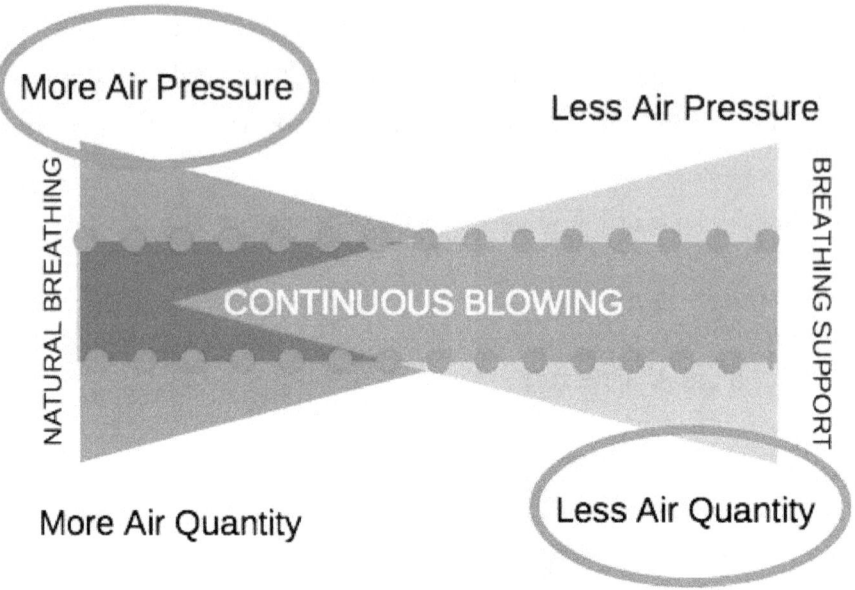

The breathing support is a firm but relaxed pressure applied by our abdominal muscles onto our diaphragm. This movement will start with little intensity but will increase towards the end in order to compensate the curve of the natural fade out.

IMPORTANT: THE BREATHING SUPPORT SHOULD NEVER INVOLVE TENSION OF THE ABDOMINAL MUSCLES. TENSION IS THE OPPOSITE OF VOCAL TECHNIQUE.

Let me give you an example so that you understand why it is so important not to tighten up your belly. Imagine trying to inflate the tires of your bike and you are using one of those manual pumpers. You pull the stick and then you push down towards the floor. When you push down, you will not

Get the FREE VIDEO TRAINING at

http://www.lornavocals.com/p/speakoutbonus

tighten up your arm, you will just go with the flow and let the momentum create the pressure of air to pump up the tires.

Now, imagine doing the same, but with your abdominal muscles. Imagine your abs as the stick of the inflator. If you tighten up your belly as if you were protecting yourself from someone who is about to punch you, you will not be able to create the required pressure. In that case, you would actually be creating a barrier.

Access the free online video that demonstrates how to perform the breathing support here: http://www.lornavocals.com/p/speakoutbonus

Some people call the abdominal breathing and the breathing support terms like "breathing with your diaphragm" or "breathing through your diaphragm". I would rather use a more accurate terminology. Actually, if you think about it, it would be impossible not involving our diaphragm when it comes to breathing. Therefore, you are always breathing with your diaphragm, whether you are using your breathing support or not.

Step 4: Resonance
In order to have a powerful voice, you need to learn how to use your resonators so that you improve your projection, avoid strain, and achieve an overall rich and beautiful sound.
When your vocal folds vibrate as the airflow goes through them, a very low volume wave sound is originated. These sound waves travel upwards through the vocal tract and, according to the position of your articulators, will be amplified in the empty chambers of your head, which work as your natural speakers.

Get the FREE VIDEO TRAINING at

http://www.lornavocals.com/p/speakoutbonus

According to the position of the articulators, the sound waves will be placed in different parts of the head, influenced by the pitch and by the intention of the speaker or singer.

Higher pitches will tend to be amplified towards the top of your head, while lower tones will tend to resonate in lower spaces such as the chest.

A common mistake is to speak or sing without leading the sound waves to resonate in the main upper chamber constituted by the sinuses. Some people let their voices trapped in their throats or in the back of their mouth. This obstructs the ideal resonance and projection of the voice.

The result of the lack of resonance in your voice will lead you to talk or sing too loud in order to be heard, but still not achieve a powerful voice. The next step of this non-balanced vocal process will be creating strain and, therefore, sustained vocal abuse.

M Exercise:

-The goal of this exercise is for you to learn how to place your voice in your "mask".

-Try to yawn, or open the internal part of your mouth as if you were yawning. This is the position of the vocal tract that you should try to maintain in the second part of this exercise.

-Breath in using your abdominal breathing.

-Hold your breath for two seconds.

-Say "m" while maintaining the expansion of the muscles inside your mouth, so that you can create as much internal space as possible.

-Start chewing to feel how the vibration of the M changes its placement through different areas of your face.

-Try to stimulate the vibration of the "m" in your "mask", which is located in your sinuses and around your nose. Avoid any tension or strain while practicing this exercise.

Get the FREE VIDEO TRAINING at

http://www.lornavocals.com/p/speakoutbonus

Access http://www.lornavocals.com/p/speakoutbonus to access a free video demonstration of this exercise.

Step 5. Pitch

Pitch is the quality of the sound that defines the frequency of the vibration of the wave and it varies from low to high. In a piano, every key has a specific pitch and it goes from low notes on the left extreme towards high notes at the right end.

The different pitches are achieved once the vocal folds stretch to different lengths according to the desired frequency. The higher the note, the more your vocal folds will be stretched. Lower notes imply the shortening of these straps of muscle.

When we try to speak in a higher pitch, our brain sends out an order that makes the cartilages attached to the vocal chords to move apart. Then, the vocal folds become thinner and tighter, and therefore, they present a stronger resistance against the airflow. This is why it is harder to sing high notes since we need to be used to the stretch, and it is also the reason why we need to be able to generate an airflow with more pressure in order to make them vibrate rapidly.

In case you do not sing, you should still create melodies with your voice, even if the pitches will not be as specific as if you were singing.

<u>In order to have a powerful voice, you need to be able to produce high and low pitches with ease.</u>

A great way to create a voice that is more engaging is by utilizing different pitches that will add color and elements of surprise to your speech.

Most of the people who have not had any vocal training are just using one or two notes while they are speaking. This translates in what is usually known as a "monotone voice". These voices are like paintings that only use a palette of two colors and that keep repeating themselves. In these cases, the result of this poor variation are presentations that can come across a not interesting enough or boring, since the audience's ears will get tired easily by the repetitive frequencies.

How to find the right pitch for your voice

Finding the right pitch and the sweet spot for your resonance will help you sound better and take better care of your voice. Frequently, the lack of awareness of the possibilities of our own voices, or trying to fit the mold of what we think our voice should sound like, ends up pushing us to force our voices into registers that are not comfortable or that can even create unnecessary strain and effort.

Some people try to sound deeper or more masculine, and then they speak way too low, not letting their voices resonate freely. Some other times, women have a voice that has an excess of high pitch frequencies and which can come across as too sharp to their audience's ears.

Finding the right spot and a comfortable register for your voice to naturally resonate will give you the possibility to eventually visit higher and lower notes that will add colors to your speech while preventing vocal abuse. A vocal coach or a phonologist will be able to help you find the sweet spot that will allow your voice to project more easily.

Slide exercise

This exercise will help you stretch your vocal folds and explore the possible pitches available to your voice.

-Breath in through your nose by using the abdominal breathing.

-Say "meeee", and start by using the lowest note available to you. Try not to move your chin down.

Get the FREE VIDEO TRAINING at

http://www.lornavocals.com/p/speakoutbonus

-Start a slide, without making any stops at any specific note and end up at your highest possible note.
-Repeat the exercise by starting in the highest possible pitch and sliding down towards your lowest pitch.

Access http://www.lornavocals.com/p/speakoutbonus to access a free video demonstration of this exercise.

IMPORTANT! READ THIS: VOCAL DISORDERS
Every week at the end of my choir class, my voice was hoarse and tired. I was 18 years old and singing as a soprano in one of my mandatory classes at the National Conservatory of Music Carlos Bouchardo, in Argentina, where I studied classical guitar. I guess they asked me to sing the soprano part just because my voice did not sound low or deep enough in order to sing the alto part.

In any case, I did not really know what I was doing. We read the melody on the chart and I was imitating my colleagues who were more experienced than me. Every time an "E" (mi) came, I knew it would be painful. It was a high note and even if I was trying my best, I kept running out of air and feeling as if someone was strangling me! Of course, I was flat. I could not hit almost any of the high notes and I knew it. I could hear the problem but I did not know how to fix it.

The choir director would give some sparse instructions about how to breathe. One day she said we needed to open up our ribs. That was a surprise! I did not even know you could "open" your ribs. I thought learning to open my ribs would be like learning how to move your stomach or something like that! It did not make any sense at all to me.

One day, one of my classmates from choir told me she went to the doctor and he told her that she was suffering from "phonatory gap" due to vocal abuse. He also explained that she needed to work on that right away before it was too late. He said that that was the reason why she was getting hoarse during and after the choir rehearsals and that it was also the reason why her voice was weak and too airy.

After she told me that, I followed her advice and I got an appointment with the ear, nose and throat doctor myself. I was not really surprised when after performing a video laryngoscopy with stroboscopy, the physician gave me the same diagnosis that my friend had received recently.

He found that, due to poor vocal technique and continuous abuse, I had a vocal disorder called phonatory gap. He said it was not very serious yet, but that I should learn how to use my voice properly before a more serious and permanent lesion was caused by the repetitive incorrect use of my vocal folds. The doctor recommended that I started a treatment with a speech therapist. I did what he said, and I had two sessions per week for two years. I rediscovered my voice and, after that, I have never had any issues in that sense again.

Do YOU have a vocal disorder?

Once you have subjected your body and your vocal folds to continuous vocal abuse, you might develop a vocal disorder. Some of the most common vocal disorders are nodules, edema and polyps, while the previous stage before the lesion is severe is called phonatory gap.

Imagine that you are using a shoe that is hurting a certain spot on your toe. The first few times you wear that shoe, the trauma will create a blister. If you insist on using the same shoe without making any changes, you will probably develop a callus instead after a few days.

The same thing happens in your vocal folds. If you get hoarse one day after abusing your voice, you might create lesions that are not too serious. If you continue hurting yourself repeatedly, your body will create a more permanent disorder. Some of these lesions can only be corrected through surgery. If you are experiencing continuous discomfort in your throat or repetitive hoarseness and these symptoms are not related to infection processes, you might have developed a vocal disorder.

Please refer to your ear, nose and throat doctor in order to perform a video laryngoscopy. This is a video exam of your vocal folds and it will determine if you have a vocal disorder. In case there is some kind of damage, the physician will recommend the best treatment, which might include surgery or speech therapy sessions.

Responsible professional vocal coaches will help you use your voice in a healthier way only in cases when there is no severe vocal disorder diagnosed by a doctor.

Get the FREE VIDEO TRAINING at

http://www.lornavocals.com/p/speakoutbonus

CHAPTER 3: YOUR NON-VERBAL COMMUNICATION

I am not good on camera and on-stage. What can I do?

<u>Being comfortable or natural on-stage or on-camera is a skill that you can certainly develop. This might require practice and the right guidance so that you can improve faster.</u>

In my early twenties, besides playing music, I used to work as a professional dancer. What started as a hobby gradually ended up becoming my main source of income while I was trying to figure out how to make a living out of music.

Even if I started dancing ballet and jazz dance as a kid, at 18 years old I got involved with a very sophisticated genre that is popular in South America: Classic Oriental Dance, which is the most artistically developed form of the modality usually known as belly dancing.

Figure. Me dancing

Because of Colombian-Lebanese singer Shakira's boom at the time, in just a few months I found myself working as a full-time instructor and choreographer, teaching more than 50 students from ages 4-65 years old. We even had TV presentations and recitals at the end of the year, which I fully produced and direct with the participation of all of my students.

In 2001, after moving to Brazil with my boyfriend at that time, I was invited to be part of the most successful professional dance group in the state of

Paraná, the "Grupo Professional de Dança do Ventre de Curitiba". We used to be booked up to perform at different events and venues in the South of Brazil. My colleagues and I were extremely serious about our art. We practiced hard and we invested heavily in pricy courses and workshops to hone our skills. Nevertheless, there was this particular girl, whom I will call Roxanna (not her real name). She was not worried at all about the quality of her dance. She was fine doing barely the minimum necessary and she would not even sweat during the shows because she was always trying to spend the least amount of energy possible.

Her dance was mediocre and she secretly knew that, just like all of us at the company thought that as well. However, the audience loved her! Even though she was not especially beautiful, and obviously not the most attractive among all the dancers on stage, she was clearly one of the favorites of the audiences. She was the best when it came to making an impression on stage! My colleagues used to say that she was great at "caras e bocas" (a Brazilian idiom that literally could be translated to "Faces and Mouths"). She was not doing much of a dance, but her facial expressions, body language, and confidence were compensating for any artistic shortage she could ever be accused of.

By mentioning this example, I am trying to prove to you how your attitude and the message sent out by your expression can be a game changer when it comes to winning an audience.

Roxana was definitely a winner and a professional entertainer. She was doing her job, but what would have happened if she would not have had such confidence in her stage presence? Certainly, she would have been kicked out of the group! Everybody, even the public without a technical knowledge about the dance, would have noticed that her artistic level was not up to standards.

Get the FREE VIDEO TRAINING at

http://www.lornavocals.com/p/speakoutbonus

I am not trying to tell you that you should just pretend you are good, and that this would be enough in order to succeed. I am trying to make a point on how just body language can be enough to give someone a great advantage that would not have been achieved otherwise especially in this case, within the competitive environment of highly trained and beautiful young dancers.

Your message without words

Even if you are not using your voice, your body is always talking and sending out a message. This communication can be so subtle that it will be performed even at a deeper level than that of the obvious movements. In the case I just commented, Roxanna was making practically the same dance steps that the rest of us at the company did, or even more basic versions of them. Nevertheless, even the simplest steps look grandiose because of her confident attitude!

According to the dictionary, non-verbal communication is communication without the spoken language, and this includes gestures, facial expressions and body movements (known collectively as "body language"), as well as unspoken understandings and presuppositions.

The challenge is that our non-verbal communication will reveal all the secrets we are desperately trying to keep to ourselves. Most of the times, unless we become really conscious about it, we end up presenting a fragmented message that is not authoritative enough or even a body language that will contradict the words we are saying.

Let's imagine you have prepared a special presentation to pitch a new project and close a great deal. The slides look great and you have included all the information needed. However, you are very nervous about it. You feel the pressure to perform, and you are secretly doubting yourself and your capacity to persuade and make the sale. You are not used to speaking in public. To be honest, you do not like it at all, but your boss asked you to do it and you could get a huge commission in case it works out.

You start your presentation, but suddenly you do not feel comfortable at all. They handed you a microphone, but since you are not familiar with using one of these devices, you awkwardly grab it. Without noticing, it was way too far from your mouth and people could not hear you. Someone in the audience asks you to put it closer to your mouth. That simple detail makes you even more nervous! Now they know you are not familiar with speaking from stage holding a microphone! However, there is no turning back. You have to carry on, and you just stand still and stiff at a specific spot in the middle of a huge stage by the whiteboard you are employing to make annotations.

Deep down, you start feeling embarrassed. You are afraid that you seem like an amateur, even if you are a professional in your field with decades of experience.

For a second, you think you will be able to get away with it. Nobody will notice you are nervous. You just have to speak like if you were talking to a client in a one-on-one meeting, and soon this will be over. The problem is, you are not confident at all that you will be able to persuade your audience to close the deal! You are too much on the spot!

Once you start feeling these emotions of insecurity and embarrassment, unless you are a trained actor, chances are, your non-verbal communication will have already revealed this lack of confidence. At this point, you feel that only a miracle could help you to regain your authority!

Basic sales psychology confirms that in order to sell your ideas, projects or even yourself, you need to be convinced internally that your product (or even you, in case you are a performer) is great and that you are positive that they will get value out of this opportunity!

Get the FREE VIDEO TRAINING at

http://www.lornavocals.com/p/speakoutbonus

You might have heard that some people will recommend that you FAKE your self-confidence. Some of them even say the phrase "fake it until you make it".

I, on the other hand, believe that you should present yourself with transparency and vulnerability in front of your audience. They will receive this message at an unconscious level and they will be a lot more likely to be impacted when they connect with the real you.

How can you get there? I invite you to give your presentation after practicing and becoming aware of your non-verbal communication. Your true connection with your mission and what you have to say will allow a more confident body language that will reinforce the importance of your words.

Mirror exercise

I love practicing in front of the mirror, and I always ask my students to do the same. Before singing in three concerts with the Symphonic Orchestra of Caxias do Sul, in Brazil, and leading more than 40 musicians on stage playing my own songs, I was very nervous.

The way I prepared myself for this important concert consisted of recording one of the rehearsals and then practicing the whole set of eleven songs in front of the mirror while wearing the same elegant dress that I would use for the actual shows! I did this every day for ten consecutive days. I danced and sang in front of the mirror holding an unplugged microphone. Little by little, I started to increasingly appreciate what I was seeing and hearing and, by getting used to it, my self-confidence started to grow.

When you get used to looking at yourself in the mirror while singing or speaking, you will start getting more comfortable with your image every day. Then you will know what everybody else sees when they are looking at you on the stage or on video.

Get the FREE VIDEO TRAINING at

http://www.lornavocals.com/p/speakoutbonus

Figure. Me singing with the Symphonic Orchestra of Caxias do Sul, Brazil.

Posture

Your posture will make a huge difference when it comes to your stage and on-camera presence, and it will also influence your image and branding even on a daily basis!

A good posture will help you breathe correctly in order to use your voice in the best possible way and it will also send out a confident message.

It is well known how our physicality can influence our state of mind and emotions. If your shoulders are down and your chest is depressed, it will be

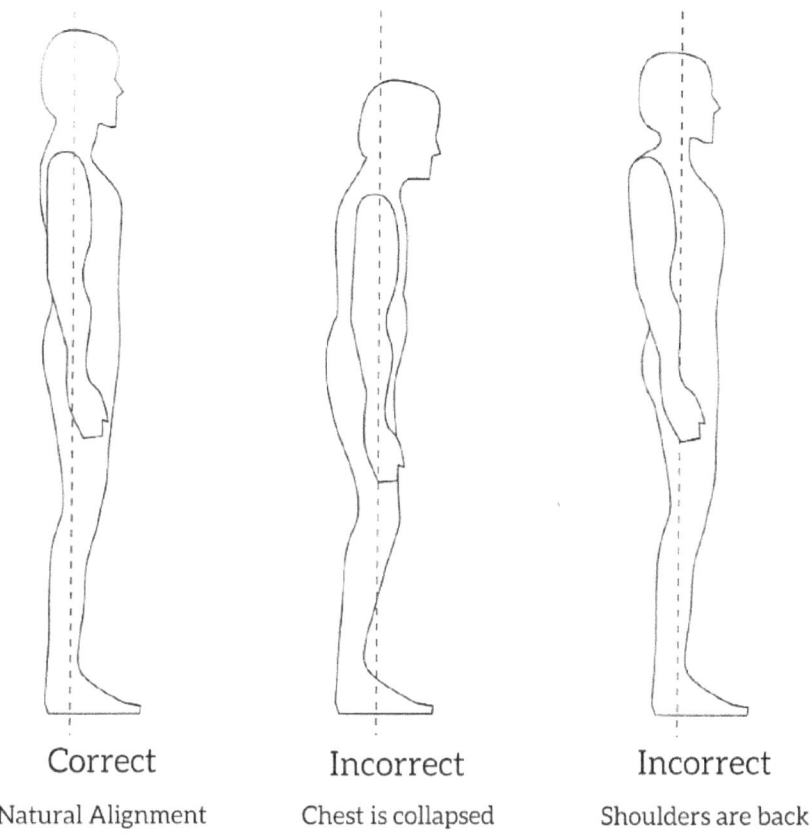

Correct	Incorrect	Incorrect
Natural Alignment	Chest is collapsed	Shoulders are back

very hard for you to have a positive energetic predisposition. Most likely, you will feel and look tired or sad.

Chances are people will unconsciously perceive you as worried or depressed, or even worse, they might think you are not feeling confident about the content of your presentation.

Have you ever noticed how great dancers usually look tall on stage, but once you see them in person they are actually pretty short or petit? This has to do with their great posture and the impact they generate through a strong stage presence!

Get the FREE VIDEO TRAINING at
http://www.lornavocals.com/p/speakoutbonus

A string on the top of your head

In any dance class, you will be asked to keep a straight and elegant posture. When I was four years old, I remember my ballet instructor always asking the students to imagine we were hanging from a string attached at the top of our heads.

Can you picture how that string would feel? Even if when you are performing as a speaker or a singer you do not necessarily need to maintain such an elongated and even unnatural position constantly, this might give you a good idea of what type of posture will improve your stage presence.

Now, experience walking around, picturing this string and taking care of your posture.

Please review some of the most common mistakes when it comes to posture, included in the following figures.

An ideal posture would allow an open chest and relaxed knees not being locked back. Before going on stage or recording on video, you can practice the relaxation sequence to help you relax your muscles and avoid unnecessary tightness.

Trying to change your posture completely in one day could be a challenge. It would even end up being counterproductive. You might feel uncomfortable and ultimately this posture would feel artificial and become unsustainable even after half an hour. Therefore, what I recommend is that you start working on improving your posture on a daily basis so that you are constantly investing in a positive body language.

If you have a hard time finding the right posture, you can always consult your physician in order to detect any additional physical causes. Practicing yoga and/or pilates will greatly help you to improve your posture and to take care of your health to prevent back pain in the future.

Get the FREE VIDEO TRAINING at

http://www.lornavocals.com/p/speakoutbonus

ON-STAGE TIP: OWN YOUR TERRITORY

One of the most common mistakes of beginning performers or speakers is their poor use of the stage space. The bigger the stage, the bigger the challenge usually gets, since a presenter with a weak presence will easily look lost unless he owns his territory.

In order to have a strong stage presence, you need to move around the stage.

Think of a wild animal, like a wolf or even try picturing a guardian's dog attitude while defending his home. All of them declare ownership of a certain piece of land that they are willing to defend and fight for. How do they show off this intention? Most likely, they will run around to cover the area. If you are presenting your work from the stage, you should never stand still in just one spot, even if there is a mic stand in the center, a podium, a whiteboard or any other device prepared for you. If you want to make a bigger impression, make sure to walk around the stage while you are speaking or singing and address different sections of the audience, while making eye contact, if possible, in different directions.

If you have the chance, try to have a conversation with the lighting crew beforehand, so that you are aware of the possibilities for you to move around without going so further away you end up in the dark. Also, try to walk the stage before the event so that you have an idea of the available space and so that you get a glimpse of how it will feel when the show starts!

Your Hands

In some countries, people are not used to engaging their hands while talking. However, some cultures, like Italian or South American, have a large repertoire of gestures that are a natural ingredient of any routine conversation.

Get the FREE VIDEO TRAINING at

http://www.lornavocals.com/p/speakoutbonus

If you are one of those who actually do not move their hands while speaking, and you are willing to create more impactful presentations, you might have to start improving this aspect as part of you communicating skills. Imagine a scene in which two people are having an argument inside a room. One of them is asking the other one to leave. In the beginning, the first person asks at a normal voice volume. Later on, after the second person does not obey, besides raising his voice, the demanding individual moves his hands and arms in the door's direction urging the unwanted visitor to get out. Obviously, his hands and arms were involved to make a stronger impression so that his message would be delivered more powerfully and obeyed.

<u>In order to deliver powerful presentations, you need to engage your whole body to communicate your ideas, especially your hands.</u>

In case you have to hold a microphone, make sure to not to grab it with both hands. This would make you look shy and insecure as if you were holding back. Instead, hold the mic in one hand and use the another one to reinforce the ideas you are exposing, while emphasizing the most important words you are willing to highlight.

If possible, always prefer to use a lavalier microphone (the one that stays attached to your clothes) or any other hands-free device. Being capable of expressing yourself with both of your hands, as opposed to holding a mic, will help you talk more naturally and allow you perform more strongly.

On Camera Tip:

If you are recording videos or broadcasting live, make sure to frame yourself in a position that includes your hands. Never leave your hands on your lap or out of the frame! Also, maintain eye contact with the lens of the camera, and never look at yourself in the monitor.

Get the FREE VIDEO TRAINING at

http://www.lornavocals.com/p/speakoutbonus

What to do with your hands

Engaging your hands will help you create the right pace for your speaking and will illustrate the ideas of the words you are saying. If you tend to speak too fast, without pauses or if you have a tendency to a monotone voice, adding hand movements will help you create the necessary rhythm to keep your listener's attention and will also give you the necessary time to organize your thoughts towards the end of each phrase.

If you are not used to engaging your hands, this might require a little practice at the beginning.

Hands Exercise

1) Get a pen

2) Hold the pen with your left hand, pretending it's a mic.

Start telling a story (it could be something simple, such as how your day was. Choose some of the most important words you consider more relevant to the story and try to make a gesture with your free hand in order to illustrate or reinforce the idea.

3) Change hands and say a couple of phrases repeating the previous step.

4) Put away the pen and continue talking engaging both hands. Make sure to synchronize the movement of your hands with the beginning and end of the words, so that your performance sends out an integrated message.

5) Experiment with the following words. Pronounce them and practice adequate gestures alternating hands and, later on, moving both hands at the same time.

Little-Big-Danger-Tiny-Mediocre-Full-Uplifting-Descending-Sunrise-Silence-Loud-Crazy-Uptight-Curious-Shy-Angry-Threat-Question

---

Get the FREE VIDEO TRAINING at

http://www.lornavocals.com/p/speakoutbonus

6) Paragraph for practice. Once you have practiced with the words, try saying the following paragraph and make one gesture for each one of the underlined words. Use the movement of your hands to pace the speed of your speech.

The night was silent. However, they could hear the coyotes further away. The day had been exhausting and they were frustrated because even though they have worked hard, they did not get any positive results. Was everything in vain? Should they go home and give up?

Your face speaks for you.

Ohmar was an excellent copywriter. He was really good at putting together the right words that would be appealing to the public in order to create promotional texts for his clients.

As a good marketer, he became aware that video is the most effective way to connect and to build an audience on social media, so he decided to begin exploring this opportunity. The only problem was that he had a hard time being on camera.

We had our first session via Skype, since he lives in Australia. Following the standard procedure with my new students, I asked him to give me a little sample of how he would perform on a Facebook Live video. In this case, I asked him to talk about how to create an appealing text for a sales letter. He accepted the challenge, and after his presentation, I could tell that he was a professional copywriter. He was very good at choosing the right words to say and he was expressing his ideas very clearly. Nevertheless, his facial expression was completely neutral, just as if we would be typing out those words as opposed to pronouncing them in front of an audience. He would keep a constant face expression all the way through. He would say "frustration" and "outstanding victory" without changing a bit.

Get the FREE VIDEO TRAINING at

http://www.lornavocals.com/p/speakoutbonus

This is why a screenwriter can not necessarily be a great actor. In theater, performers train themselves to add their emotions and personal interpretation of the words to the script, by using their body language in order to move the spectators. If the actors are not capable of connecting to their own emotions while saying their lines, they will not be able to win the audience.

Let's take a test. Say the following pairs of words in front of a mirror:

Sad- Happy
Small-Big
Hot-Cold
Curious-Boring

How did it go? Were you able to include some extra interpretation to the sole sound of these terms? Or did you have an unaltered facial expression all the way through?

I am not asking you to suddenly change the way you speak and start acting exaggeratedly. This would feel fake and it would backfire on you. Your audience would get that forced unnatural attitude right away.

What I am asking of you is to start practicing a new engagement of your facial expressions in order to support your message.

If you feel you are overreacting, don't worry. This is just an exercise. We always practice "over the top" so that once you have experienced this new concept, you can integrate it while speaking naturally.

IMPORTANT: If you still feel that exploring new facial expressions does not feel natural to you, don't try it in front of an audience yet, otherwise you will come across as if you were "pretending" or "posing". For now, keep experimenting in private and run some tests recording yourself on

Get the FREE VIDEO TRAINING at
http://www.lornavocals.com/p/speakoutbonus

video. Gradually, you will find the right way to integrate these new ideas in order to create more powerful presentations.

Click here to access the free sequence video exercises
http://www.lornavocals.com/p/speakoutbookbonus

Your dress code speaks for you

As a former professional dancer and singer, every time I think of being on stage or on video, the first thing I think of is: What am I going to wear? Actually, wardrobe, hair, and makeup are essential when you are building your brand in order to create a great first impression. Making a mistake in this sense can truly ruin things if you are overdressed, underdressed or if you just did not make the smartest choice while getting ready.

In 2011, when I recorded the first version of my Vocal Method for Singers in Portuguese (Fundamentals of Vocal Technique Volume 1 and 2), I headed by myself for ten days to the recording studio. Early in the morning, wearing some of my nicest outfits and not having anybody to assist me in this sense, I thought that showing up, talking in front of the camera and sharing great content would be enough.

To my surprise, when I went back to watch the recorded material, I was extremely disappointed. I could notice my hair looking messy and some makeup flaws. I found that the outfit I was wearing did not look professional at all and that it was too colorful, considering the background of the studio where I had been shooting.

Therefore, I decided to delete everything and start from scratch! I called Hayet el Nil (https://www.facebook.com/iracecristina.almeida), one of my best friends who happens to be an extremely talented fashion designer and who has amazing skills when it comes to makeup and hair styling. I asked for her help while I was recording and to take care of my overall image. We negotiated a price I could afford and we started over.

I explained to her the idea behind the vocal method, who my audience was and what message I was trying to communicate with this project as a whole. We also talked about my clothes, colors, and makeup preferences. I did not want to create a character for this production. I just wanted to appear as the BEST VERSION OF MYSELF.

Once she got the idea, we put together some possible combinations of wardrobe and make up for the different moments of the recording. For example, when it was the time to show the movements of the ribs for the rib abdominal breathing, I was wearing a tight black top with some loose black pants in order to show the movement. When it was time to wrap up the program, I was wearing a fancier white dress.

She also proposed different looks for my hair and makeup.

While I was filming, she was there all along, making sure that there were no loose ends, that my makeup was not blurry, and that my bra was not showing. Hiring her was the best choice I could have made! It saved me time and it helped me relax and focus solely on my job, which was speaking to the camera. I did not have to worry about my looks!

If you are planning on making a presentation or a video recording, I highly recommend you decide what your wardrobe will be in advance. Most of us need a second opinion on this matter, so I encourage you to ask for somebody else's assistance. You can also take pictures of yourself with the different options and take a look at them afterward. Waiting for a few days before revising the photos will be best to guarantee a fresh look on the matter.

For example, I like to shoot educational videos at my professional studio with a white background. After recording dozens of videos, I have noticed

---

Get the FREE VIDEO TRAINING at

http://www.lornavocals.com/p/speakoutbonus

that some colors work better than others, and the same thing happens with colors of lipstick and different hairstyles.

Sometimes a small detail, like using a nude lipstick instead of a red one can influence the message I am trying to convey. While a red lipstick will work best while I am singing a song or recording a singing tutorial, a more conservative lip color will help me come across as a more mature and professional consultant when I am talking in a business environment.

In order to have a powerful presence and deliver your message with persuasion, choose your wardrobe wisely in order to create a consistent branding. Always consider the possibility of investing in an image consultant.

Get the FREE VIDEO TRAINING at
http://www.lornavocals.com/p/speakoutbonus

CHAPTER 4: HOW TO MASTER YOUR WORD CHOICE AND WORD PERFORMANCE

Words that matter

I have heard many times the statement that when you are speaking in public, the words you say produce only ten percent of your results, while the other 90 percent will be carried through your non-verbal communication. Nevertheless, that theory, which has even been confirmed by several studies, has never made real sense to me.

As a performer, I would prefer to find words that are effective and powerful as sharp arrows hitting the target of the audience I am trying to connect with!

Therefore, in this chapter, I invite you to explore the best ways to find the words that will make a difference every time you are presenting your work. The words of a strong performer should not be overlooked as a matter of secondary importance. If you want to be a persuasive speaker, your words should be one of your superpowers!

Get the FREE VIDEO TRAINING at

http://www.lornavocals.com/p/speakoutbonus

Speak as if you were writing a hit song

A great song always tells a story that the listeners can relate to in an emotional way. We tend to give lyrics a personal interpretation that moves us because of our own life experiences. Maybe a romantic ballad expresses the deep feelings we have towards our significant one. A fun upbeat tune can inspire us to keep on going while working out at the gym.

I have been writing songs since I was eight years old, I have earned a diploma in Journalism and I got my Bachelor's Degree in Songwriting while studying in Los Angeles, California. I have always been fascinated by words and writing, while I am an avid reader in Spanish (I was born in Argentina), English (I was raised as bilingual since my father's family is British) and Portuguese (I lived in Brazil for 11 years).

Since I work as a trilingual voice coach and songwriter, I switch between languages several times in the same day while working with clients from all over the world. I also create songs for commercial and artistic use in Hollywood TV and Film productions as part of the team of one of the leading music publishing and licensing companies in Los Angeles, Latin Music Specialists.

Some people ask me in what language do I think or dream. I usually answer that at first, before verbalizing my ideas, I come up with an intention of what I am about to say. Only in a posterior moment, which could be less than a second afterward, according to the situation, I find the right expressions to communicate my message in either English, Spanish or Portuguese. I am never entirely identified with any of these languages, and I have traces of different accents in the three of them! What I am trying to tell you is that no matter the language you speak, you will find the most effective words to say if you explore your internal world and the sensations of your body. This is what we always do when we write songs.

Get the FREE VIDEO TRAINING at

http://www.lornavocals.com/p/speakoutbonus

During my university training as a songwriter, I found several common grounds between the advanced techniques to write lyrics, and copywriting (specialized marketing and sales composition).

Both modalities recommend that you take advantage of the use of the senses: touch, smell, hearing, sight, and taste, as the most effective way of creating an impact and connecting with the listeners.

The effective use of stories, metaphors, and analogies appeal to body sensations and deep emotions that activate each of your listener's memories in a unique and personal way. This process creates a bond between you and your audience.

Object Writing Exercise

The goal of object writing is to work out your creative muscle so that you can explore an infinite variety of ideas that include sensations and emotions. You will get the best results if you practice this exercise every day, first thing in the morning.

I have learned this with Daniel Indart. He is one of my former teachers and a successful songwriter and music producer who has written hundreds of tunes for big Hollywood movie productions. Some examples of his work can be found in films with A-list stars such as Tom Cruise and Clint Eastwood, and also in several popular tv series such as Narcos, Jane the Virgin, CSI, and Dexter, among many others.

-Choose a different object every day. Start by selecting something concrete such as one of the material objects that are in the room. It could be a pencil, the rug, the chair you are sitting on or the T-shirt you are wearing.

- Set the timer on your cell phone to ring after 10 minutes. Shut down all distractions and grab a pen and paper.

Get the FREE VIDEO TRAINING at

http://www.lornavocals.com/p/speakoutbonus

- Start by writing whatever comes to your mind while trying to describe the object. Use the different senses (sight, smell, touch, hear and taste), in order to describe, from different perspectives, the object you choose to talk about. It could be something like this in case you are writing about a rug.

"The rug tastes like dirt and sand and my tongue gets dry while I lick it. It is rough and soft at the same time. I feel the tingling in my fingertips if I caress it softly. It looks like those expensive articles you see in fancy decoration magazines, but it smells like cat litter, reminding me that it is one of the cat Tom's favorite spots in the house..." etc.

- Keep going for ten minutes. Don't judge, don't stop and don't try to make it perfect. It is what it is, and its spontaneity is the most important value you will get out of it.
- Once the timer is done, stop. Close your notebook, or throw the paper in the trash. It does not matter. The exercise is done for the day. Go on with your daily routine.
- Repeat the exercise every morning. After the second week, you will be AMAZED at how easily new ideas will start flowing!

This is part of the essential training of a songwriter and this ensures that you will be ready to go at any time when you need to come up with some new work! It will empower you since you will no longer be relying on "random inspiration". The object writing exercise is a workout that will add to your creativity and word choice when speaking, even in improvisation settings.

The best thing about it is that it is not a formula that you need to memorize in order to hypnotize your audience. It is the development of your inner creative potential as a human being.

Get the FREE VIDEO TRAINING at

http://www.lornavocals.com/p/speakoutbonus

I use the object writing exercise every time I need to write a new song. I start with an idea, or maybe a scene or certain situation I want to write lyrics about, and then I just let the words flow on paper for a couple of pages. Once I feel I have enough, I go back and read it to find the strongest expressions among everything I have written down. Usually, out of this object writing exercise, I get the main phrases, images or expressions that will lead me to finish a whole song.

<u>In order to present yourself powerfully in front of your audience, practice the object writing exercise as often as possible. It will help you find great ideas that you can include in your speech afterward and it will also hone your skills by conditioning yourself to explore words that relate to the senses.</u>

Storytelling

A great way to enrich your talk is to include stories that tell something about you or your experience and which prove the point you are trying to make about the topic you are discussing.

Stories have been utilized as the most effective tool for lecturing, even when the written word did not exist. Fairytales, the Bible, mythology from different cultures and even the movies from nowadays, among thousands of other examples, use stories as the most powerful vehicle to make a statement. After all, we all have stories to tell and we all enjoy stories! As a good speaker, by taking advantage of this, you will work out your capacity of creating suspense and anticipation while narrating experiences that will clearly reinforce your perspective on the topic you are discussing or the project you are representing.

Exercising your creativity and your resourcefulness with words through the object writing exercise will help you enrich your narration with details.

Get the FREE VIDEO TRAINING at

http://www.lornavocals.com/p/speakoutbonus

These details are essential in order to create engagement and connection with your audience. Make sure that you explore and take advantage of those small observations since they are golden moments that will become memorable for your audience. They will keep your spectators at the edge of their seats and usually open up a space for the laughs or the sighs.

Therefore, always MAKE SURE TO INCLUDE A STORY! This can be an example of something that happened to you and that explains why you came to the conclusions you are presenting. It could be a comment about the story behind a song you will perform next, or it can be the transformation one of your clients went through by applying the principles you are demonstrating.

Always have your story ready! I have used several stories in this book so that you can understand where I come from. This is the real stuff. Some of these situations were extremely stressful at the time when I was experiencing them.

Actually, opening up about facts that were unpleasant or that show our imperfections or our evolution will create an even stronger impression and connection. These stories could be secrets that you would never have wanted anybody to know about!

When I started studying vocals, I was a poorly skilled singer. The worst part was that while I was struggling, I got kicked out of the choir because I was not good enough! I was 18 years old and, for me, that was extremely traumatic.

After many years of training, I became a professional singer and people started to respect my work and make compliments about my talent. Nevertheless, I was always trying to hide this dark spot on my resume, and I would never have thought of mentioning it to anybody! I thought if people knew about it, it would make me look bad. I thought my humble beginnings would damage my image as a musician.

Get the FREE VIDEO TRAINING at

http://www.lornavocals.com/p/speakoutbonus

Nevertheless, when I started studying online marketing, in 2013, I was introduced to a whole new paradigm on how to promote my products. At the time, I had my own vocal method which I had released as a two-part collection of DVDs with my vocal program for singers. I had already been selling my courses online with a moderate social media success. My YouTube channel and my Facebook Fanpage were doing okay and I became pretty good at ranking on Google for my niche. For more than five years I managed to make a living teaching singing by getting students who would find me organically through Google and YouTube search, without spending a dime on paid traffic!

When I moved to Los Angeles, I was ready to take a step further and I started studying and investing heavily on programs by marketers as Chalene Johnson, Brendon Burchard, Jeff Walker, James Wedmore and many others. To my surprise, I fell in love with their perspective on marketing!

As a journalist graduate, I had the obsolete idea of a dichotomy when it came to communication. In my head, I unconsciously believed that there was something evil about promoting products. In my ignorant prejudiced mind, "marketing equaled advertising", and "advertising equaled lies or sugar coating". On the other hand, journalism was supposed to representing the truth about the facts.

I was soooo wrong! Thanks to the thought leaders I just mentioned, I understood that the best I could do in order to build my brand and my business would be to market myself as who I truly was! I understood the power of showing my vulnerability and the importance of integrity in order to create influence.

I started creating new videos to promote the singing program that I was selling to my Brazilian audience at that time. I did not have any professional equipment, and I really did not know anybody who could assist me in that matter in Los Angeles.

Get the FREE VIDEO TRAINING at

http://www.lornavocals.com/p/speakoutbonus

Following Chalene's advice, I made it happen with what I had! I went to my room and shot a 3-part video series about how to sing better.

I did not have too much space at my first Hollywood apartment, so I used a 10-dollar tripod holding my iPhone 5 on top of the bed! I used a microphone that I had for recording vocals and I shot a 20-minute lesson to answer the question everybody seemed to be asking me when I told them I was a vocal instructor. People usually inquires: Can anybody learn how to sing?

In that video lesson, I explained mostly the content I deliver in my introductory classes, which includes a version of the five steps that I mentioned in chapter 2 this book, which is about voice. The main difference was that, for the first time, I included stories of MY OWN frustrations and failures along the way, in order to illustrate the transformation I had gone through thanks to vocal technique. Among other stories, I included the one about my vocal disorder, my insecurities, and the shame I experienced when I was kicked out of the choir.

I uploaded the three videos on my YouTube channel as "unlisted", with the intention to deliver them solely to those who would sign up providing their email for my free program. I set up the system and I thought everything was great.

A couple of months afterward, I noticed an extreme increase in my social media following and engagement. It was working! People actually started to buy more. For some reason, I visited my YouTube channel. To my surprise, the first video I recorded, the one I just told you about in which I narrated my embarrassing frustrations before learning to sing, had literally EXPLODED. I had not noticed that instead of keeping the video "unlisted", I uploaded the video as "public" and everybody could see it. It went viral! I had never seen so many comments, likes, and shares. In a month I had reached hundreds of thousands of views, while my channel had grown

---

Get the FREE VIDEO TRAINING at

http://www.lornavocals.com/p/speakoutbonus

more than 5X from a couple of thousands of subscribers to more than 10k!

There were also beautiful comments of people who were saying that after watching that video had decided to pursue their dreams. Most of them were talking about how they felt relieved when I opened up about the obstacles I encountered on my way to becoming a professional singer!

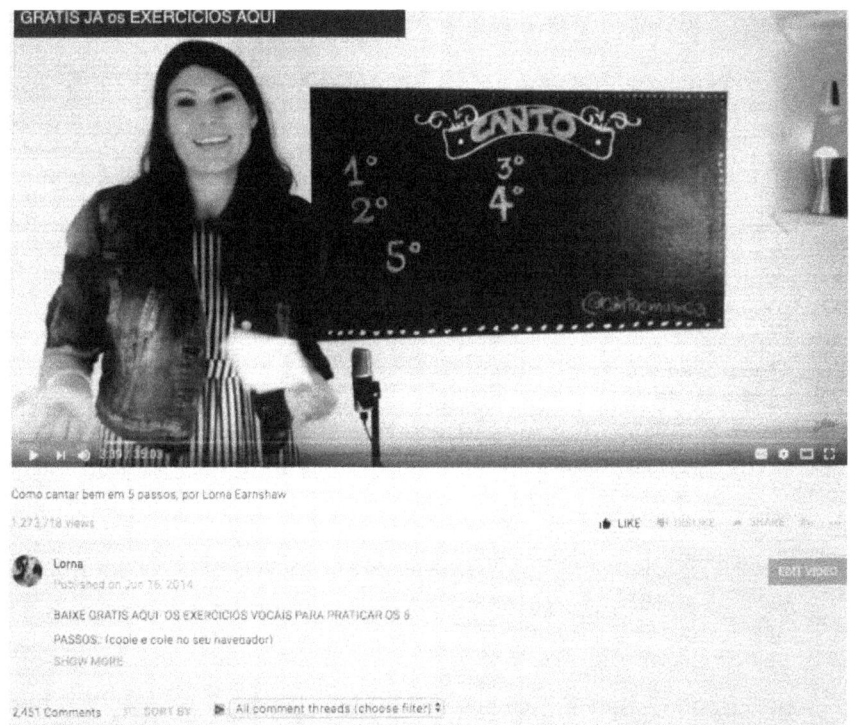

Figure. One of my most popular videos on YouTube

This video that I posted by accident, has been my most viewed video on YouTube, with more than 1.27 million views as of March 2018. In this video, I included a link to my free program and mainly because of it I was able to cover around 80% of my basic bills living in Los Angeles for four years! I am talking about making around U$S 100,000!

Get the FREE VIDEO TRAINING at

http://www.lornavocals.com/p/speakoutbonus

What is YOUR story?

Now, I would like you to think of at least three stories that you can include in your presentations. I am POSITIVE that you have many more than three. Please be honest and open up. Think about that one thing that you are even uncomfortable to talk about. Write it down. Do some object writing. Try to find what the strongest message is that each of those stories represents and find the right moment or subject in your talk to include it.

If you are an author, you need a story to talk about YOUR transformation and YOUR "why". This is the most powerful marketing tool that will define your brand. This is what real connection is about. This is speaking out by being yourself!

Some of the most successful thought leaders use their main story and repeat it every time they go on stage.

If you are familiar with Brendon Burchard, I am sure you have heard about his car accident story dozens of times, as myself! Honestly, I do not get tired of listening to that story. I always get moved while he relates the details of a situation in which he almost died and after which he woke up to the realization of the importance of living a meaningful life.

In order to have a powerful presence and to connect to your audience by being who you are, define your main story, a story that reveals not only your victories but also your struggles and vulnerability.

Once you have written down the main idea of this essential story, and after doing some object writing in order to include details that relate to the senses, you can record yourself narrating it as if you were talking to a friend. Then, listen back to it. Even better, you can share this story with a friend without letting him know in advance that this is part of the content creation of your presentation. After all, the idea is that you practice your speaking

---

Get the FREE VIDEO TRAINING at

http://www.lornavocals.com/p/speakoutbonus

skills so that you can talk in front of an audience with the same confidence you would talk to a friend.

Analogies

After being a teacher for more than 15 years, I had developed my capacity to explain concepts that otherwise would sound way too abstract. Trying to understand and explain to my students how our voices work has been my main mission and one of my trademarks that differentiates my work from other vocal instructors.

Before teaching, I struggled to understand why I had to practice certain exercises and I had never really comprehended the complex mechanism of our voices. However, when I started to make a living out of singing lessons, I made sure to study how this physiology worked while helping my students understand why I was asking them to perform all the weird noises and movements that are part of the vocal practice.

As a personal trait, even if I consider myself quite emotional, I need to analyze things in order to process them. If a concept does not make sense to me, it will be extremely hard to memorize the data. For example, I have never been able to remember the names of the muscles and different parts of the larynx. Trust me, I have tried. I can remember them for a couple of days, and then I forget again! Actually, I am not very worried about all those details, because I know that my clients will not get value or a significant transformation out of them.

Instead of showing off by naming complicated muscles, I am inclined to find simple explanations for the various processes. These are analogies that I have found to efficiently illustrate the main idea that will help my students to recreate the movements that otherwise would be hard to describe. You can find some examples of these analogies in chapter 2 of this book. One

---

Get the FREE VIDEO TRAINING at

http://www.lornavocals.com/p/speakoutbonus

of them is the use of the idea of the tire inflator when demonstrating the principle of the breathing support in the abdominal breathing.

Analogies exercise:

List the most crucial ideas you intend to explain during your presentation. These are the concepts that will influence your audience to understand the importance or the utility of what you are representing. If you are a coach and you are speaking about how you can train your mind to create new habits, you can use the example of how you could train a kid and teach him to go to sleep early and not watching tv until late at night. You can show the similarities of the difficulties and the resistance you will face at the beginning until the new routine has been accepted as a natural part of the day. This is a logical process. Nobody would deny that even the most stubborn kid would be able to create a new habit if the parents consistently insist on molding the new conditioning. Therefore, your audience will most likely accept this concept as true or, at least, possible.

Once you have established the correlation and the common ground between the previous undeniable example and the new idea you are bringing up to the table, the concept that you are willing to convey will be more easily accepted.

<u>In order to communicate with influence, prepare analogies that will reinforce the main points that you want to deliver in your talk.</u>

Start by building your authority: bio-statement

If for some reason we were talking in a social setup and without being introduced to each other beforehand, we started discussing vocal technique, you would listen to me and assume that I have studied the subject. Nevertheless, until I actually have explained to you who I am and what my experience is, you probably would not take me too seriously.

Get the FREE VIDEO TRAINING at

http://www.lornavocals.com/p/speakoutbonus

Let's imagine you have heard some comments that are contrary to the main principles I teach. A good example could be the affirmation that not everybody can learn how to sing.

You could tell me, "I will never be able to speak in public, I don't have the gift". Then I would say, "of course you can learn!". But you would still not hear me. Then I could say: "I am a trilingual voice coach and I have already helped more than 55,000 people free their voices through my internet lessons, and more than 350 students in my private sessions for the past 15 years. I have never met any student who hasn't got results with my method". What would you say after that? At least, that would actually get your attention and stimulate you to review your old beliefs!

This is why you need to create your bio statement! This is a phrase or a couple of phrases of not more than three lines which defines what you do and that includes some type of social proof (if you can include numbers, that would be even better!).

After refining it, you will be able to adapt it to every specific situation. For example, since I work with speakers and as a trainer for business presentations, I could adjust the bio statement to provide information that would make sense according to the specific audience I am addressing.

If I am teaching on how to get people to watch your videos on YouTube, I could include in my bio statement that as for March 2018 I have reached almost four million views on my YouTube channel. In case I am teaching vocal technique, it would be more relevant to mention that I have enrolled more than 850 students in my online singing program.

Exercise: Create your bio statement now

-Start with your name: " Hi! I'm (name)

Get the FREE VIDEO TRAINING at

http://www.lornavocals.com/p/speakoutbonus

-Write down the most relevant and impressive information related to the audience you will be addressing. Include the main benefit of your product or mission of your work. Add one variation.

Examples: Hi! I am..........(your name), author of the bestseller book ......
(or) I have already (taught) (number of people) to (the transformation you offer)

.....I have already raised more than five million dollars in revenue by investing in real state....

.... For the last twenty years, I have helped people to find balance and happiness in their lives....

- Repeat the statement until you memorize it! This is crucial! You need to say these sentences with total confidence and without even thinking about it. Hesitation while pronouncing this statement would completely neutralize its effect.

- Use this statement every time you start recording a video, especially for social media. Of course, use your discretion to decide in which situations it would be appropriate and relevant.

Speak your audience's language

When you are creating your content, it is extremely important that you employ the words and expressions your ideal audience would use to refer to the topic you are exploring. This will allow you to connect with them faster and it will build your authority so that they understand that you know how to provide them with what they need.

Get the FREE VIDEO TRAINING at
http://www.lornavocals.com/p/speakoutbonus

IMPORTANT:
The more accurately you are capable of describing your audience's pain points, the more likely you will be perceived as an authority capable of providing the solution.

Have you ever heard someone speaking and then you thought: "wow, it seems like this talk is just about me!". Maybe, while you were listening to a speaker's keynote, you resonated with him just because he was able to put in words exactly the way you feel. It seemed like he was talking directly to you or about you! This is the power of a word choice that includes terms that are relatable to your public!

Sometimes, especially when we are experts in our field and we have a considerable amount of knowledge around a certain topic, we tend to use words that would never be mentioned by our public.

For example, in 2012, when I released my first product for online selling, I named it "Fundamentals of Vocal Technique". I was very proud of that name. I thought it was a fancy title for my singing vocal method! For sure, it was professional, accurate and academic. It would have been the perfect name for one of the classes of a Vocal Performance program at any university.

However, nobody searches "Fundamentals of Vocal Technique" on Google if they want to learn how to sing or if they are looking for a solution or a course to buy! That is why, when I released the digital version of this program I changed the title to a Brazilian translation that goes more or less like this: "How to sing better-online course". Simple and direct.

Therefore, this is a very important reason why you should always include your audience's most common expressions in your presentation, videos or any other type of content.

Your target audience is right now browsing on Google to find someone who can help them, and when they do, they do not usually know what the solution to their problem is. They just know the "symptoms", or perhaps they have the end result in mind but they do not know what the actual tool that will solve their issues is.

Before studying with me, most of my clients did not know how powerful vocal technique exercises would be in order to help them to achieve their singing dreams. I can assure you that most of them were quite discouraged about their voices, so they were not out there looking to sign up for a program to practice breathing exercises.

Choosing to use my audience's terminology helped me get more visibility for my videos and for all of my promotional content. Also, I used the title "5 steps to sing better" to name my most viewed videos on my YouTube channel, the one that today has more than 1.3 million views. I am positive that if I would have named that video "5 fundamentals of vocal technique", only a few people would have seen it!

Once my potential students are watching my videos, I have the opportunity to describe the feelings and emotions they are experiencing while going through the issue I can help them with. Later on, I can present my solution which this time may include some more sophisticated terms. I once heard someone saying that you have to offer your audience "what they want, and then give them what they need".

By following this process, you are being honest and you are actually taking them by the hand while subtly overcoming their resistance. You are embracing your responsibility as a thought leader by providing the right answer to their needs. It works like a good doctor who can prescribe you the right medication because he is familiar with the symptoms you are experiencing.

Get the FREE VIDEO TRAINING at
http://www.lornavocals.com/p/speakoutbonus

TIP: Make sure to take note of the words and expressions that your clients, friends and the audience you are addressing use when talking about their challenges. A great idea is to run surveys every time you have the chance and include their textual answers in your presentations.

For instance, when people sign up for a first consultation with me, I ask them to fill in a form which includes the following questions: "What is your main challenge when it comes to … ","What are you looking for in this first consultation?" Only these two answers will provide you with enough words and ideas! The phrases they include in their answers will also work great as part of the text for your sales pages.

Hmmm, ahhh, just like fillers!

Fillers are those words, syllables or even isolated vowels that we use and which do not have a specific meaning or a function within the phrases. Every time you say "ahhhh" "mmmm" or even when you use "I mean" or "just like" unnecessarily and repetitively, you are filling an empty space. This usually happens when you are trying to find the right words to express yourself or while you are scanning around with your eyes, in order to end your sentences. The problem is that, when you utilize fillers excessively, you might look as if you were trying to figure out what to say next. This will hurt your credibility and will weaken your image.

Frequently, we use fillers because we have a hard time organizing the ideas in our heads and preparing the whole sentences before starting to talk. We might be speaking too fast, or we might get distracted and lose the thread of what we were saying. Then, a filler avoids the silence and the discomfort that we would feel if we left the audience hanging!

The use of fillers is usually related with the anxiety and excessive speed of our speech. It could also have to do with some lack of focus or with distractions as a result of negative self-talk!

Get the FREE VIDEO TRAINING at

http://www.lornavocals.com/p/speakoutbonus

How can you train to eliminate fillers? First, it would be great if you could examine yourself when you are speaking by listening back to your recordings. Identify what fillers you use and in which specific situation you are employing them.

Then, try to speak more slowly and give yourself time to think about the words you want to say. If you need to stop to think and find the right word, do so! Simply pause and sustain your look in the same spot you were looking at before the pause. Don't look around the room for ideas. For sure, the right word will not materialize in front of your eyes! (just kidding!)

Continue talking and finish the sentence once you have decided what words to say next. Little by little, you will get used to finding the right pace and to organize the structure of your phrases in advance. With time, this process will get faster, and before you know it, you will have significantly diminished the number of fillers.

In the meantime, you will be playing and experimenting with the power of the pause.

The power of the pause

The symphonic orchestra is playing a fast movement of a symphony by Beethoven. All groups of instruments are engaged in a crescendo. Suddenly, the maestro makes a rapid move and conducts the musicians to stop. For a couple of seconds, the pause is the protagonist. There is tension, mystery, and curiosity. The audience is waiting for the resolution.

As a trained musician, I have learned that there is POWER in a pause. A short silence to separate your ideas or certain words can renew your audience's interest. It can refresh their ears and it can give them a break to absorb all the sounds that have previously been played.

When you make a pause, you are creating suspense and you are giving extra importance to whatever you will say next.

Get the FREE VIDEO TRAINING at

http://www.lornavocals.com/p/speakoutbonus

<u>In order to have a powerful presence, you need to OWN the power of your pauses.</u>

Sometimes, speaking way too fast or without pauses will come out as a response to nervousness or lack of confidence. It may seem like we are trying to prove ourselves, and therefore we keep on throwing new ideas to the public in order to make a point.

Nevertheless, most of the times, expressing ideas in a more succinct way, and highlighting the most important concepts with previous and following pauses will create a stronger effect and will work better to build your credibility and authority when speaking to an audience.

Watch a comedian's act. They have mastered the power of the pause. They make a joke and they stop. That moment is when they throw the ball to the audience so that they can really engage in the conversation by laughing. Good comedians are confident that their jokes will work, and most of the times, they have tested them out previously. They are expecting the positive reaction of the audience, and when they make a pause while usually striking a pose, they are commanding and conducting, just as a maestro conducts the orchestra.

Once I was at church and I had the opportunity to compare two presentations of the same sermon by the pastor. I went to the first gathering, and on my way out I ended up meeting up with some friends who were volunteering at the second gathering.

The pastor, who is also a writer and speaker, is very experienced and he has a strong stage presence. You can tell that some of his followers are actually his fans.

In the first presentation, at the morning service, he made a joke by commenting on some situation with his wife. It was actually very funny. He

---

Get the FREE VIDEO TRAINING at

http://www.lornavocals.com/p/speakoutbonus

made a pause and I, as most of the audience, laughed. After some people even clapped, he moved on to deliver his message.

On the other hand, during the second presentation, he repeated, almost identically, his first speech of the day. Silently, I was waiting for the funny joke. However, he said the words really fast and moved on to the following idea. This time, he missed the chance to win the audience! By not making the pause in the same spot as he did in the morning, he conducted people to keep moving on until the next pause, which is why nobody laughed this time! Not even one person. Because he was moving forward, everybody was moving forward with him.

That day, I was not working or coaching, nevertheless, my innocence and my attitude as a common listener gave me the opportunity to prove, once again, how the expectation a presenter creates through a pause can serve as a command to influence his audience's reaction.

Pause Exercise:

- Record yourself speaking about your topic for a minute. Listen back. Did you use pauses? Did you give your listeners a break to integrate what they had just heard before bombarding them with the next concept? Were you linking all the phrases or breathing at random moments in the middle of the sentences?

Now, try again. Think of the words that are the most important. Practice creating a pause before and/or after them.

Example of the use of the pause as a way to highlight words:

The solution is *(pause)* consistency. *(pause)* (Development or example of the idea)

or

The solution *(pause)* is *(pause)* consistency. (Development or example of the idea)

The bottom line is we should never feel uncomfortable when there is a short silence. If you are in charge, you are setting the rules and leading the conversation. You are taking your time and you have the authority to gently conduct your audience like the male should conduct his female partner while dancing the tango!

The strategy of owning the power of your pause is effective in any setup. It could also define your influence in negotiations, social meetups or even in a family environment.

Your speaking rhythm

By listening back to some of your recordings, you will be able to analyze the rhythm and the speed of your talk. Why did I mention rhythm and speed as two different things? Because I am using musical concepts.

The speed of a song has to do with the tempo, which is the number of beats per minute that dictate the periodic beats of a music piece. All the beats are equal, and you can speed up or slow down the tune by modifying this parameter.

On the other hand, the rhythm has a design on its own, it combines strong beats and weak beats in different manners so that that specific piece of music has a certain characteristic.

Therefore, you will be able to recognize the salsa rhythm as opposed to the polka rhythm or the waltz rhythm. Nevertheless, even slightly speeding up or slowing down the tempo of those rhythms, you will still probably be able to identify them as waltz or polka.

When you are speaking, your voice is performed in a specific period of time. If you think you have a monotone voice or someone has told you so, chances are your voice does not have rhythm, while it simply maintains a certain constant speed. It could be fast or slow, but it does not create groove or engagement.

Get the FREE VIDEO TRAINING at
http://www.lornavocals.com/p/speakoutbonus

The problem when you are not creating that groove is that your voice will not have the element of surprise to capture your listeners' attention. Naturally, their tendency will be to zoom out after a while. Imagine a symphony in which all the movements have the same speed. Or imagine a rock concert in which all the songs use the same tempo. Probably, the presentation would get boring and the performers would lose their audience's attention right away. That is the reason why every band strategically creates their setlist with the songs they will perform in order to present a variety that will maintain the audience's interest. Experienced musicians will alternate fast and slow songs in order to create different atmospheres during their concert. How can you apply that musical idea to make your voice more interesting and so that you can deliver your message with more authority and influence? You need to integrate the meaning of the words you say, by combining their speed and rhythm with the intonation and the emotional content that will reinforce the ultimate significance of the concepts you are sharing.

Word performance

What is the difference between a good actor and a bad actor interpreting the same script? The good actor performs his lines by increasing the content and adding extra value. He pours his internal world into the scene in order to move the audience. When the good actor gives life to a character, he connects with his own emotions first to allow the public to resonate with them.

<u>In order to deliver an impactful performance, you have to connect with your listeners at an emotional level.</u>

When you add passion to your words and different moods, you are enhancing your message so that every sentence will have a multiplied power. If you open your heart, many people will open their hearts to you as well.

Get the FREE VIDEO TRAINING at

http://www.lornavocals.com/p/speakoutbonus

If you have a monotone voice, you are probably saying all the words with a very similar intonation and timber. If you have not had the opportunity to explore different sounds of your own voice, you might engage your default vocal setup.

By practicing the following exercises, we will explore different options that you can add to your voice repertoire in order to get new colors for your palette of possibilities!

Subtle changes in your voice might express different meanings for exactly the same sequence of words. In those cases, you could only verify the difference between various possible speaker's intentions through oral communication.

Mood variations

Here is an example of how the same words can carry at least four different meanings according to your interpretation. Let's explore the combination of the words "You"+"Did" in their interrogative form.

	Meaning
You did?	Very surprised
You did?	Curious
You did?	In agreement
You did?	Angry

Dynamics Variations

One of the characteristics and parameters which you can utilize in order to create different nuances for your voice has to do with the dynamics.

A sound can be forte (high intensity) or piano (low intensity). These two terms come from Italian and are used in traditional music notation.

Get the FREE VIDEO TRAINING at
http://www.lornavocals.com/p/speakoutbonus

Let's experience the difference between saying the following words with opposite dynamics.

a) Secret (forte version) and Secret (piano version)

b) Scream (forte version) and Scream (piano version)

Which version made more sense according to the intrinsic meaning of each word?

Pitch and phrases melody

Your intonation, which is the pitch direction and emphasis of your sentences will define different messages that might even sound contradictory if not applied accordingly to your intentions.

Every language has its own intonation characteristics according to regional accents. Therefore, by listening to the melody and the pitch when a person is talking, you can be able to identify where this person is originally from. People from New Zealand will apply a different intonation to their words than a person from Great Britain, even if both of them are speaking English. Also, you can notice a different melody while two individuals say the same words if one is originally from the south of the US while the other one is from the West Coast.

The same rule applies to every language. Spanish from Spain has a different melody than Spanish from Argentina.

Therefore, there is not a unique correct way to define the intonation of your speaking. Nevertheless, make sure that the melody and the pitch you are using are supporting the message you want to deliver so that you can transmit certainty and confidence about your subject.

Generally, ending phrases in an ascending way will correspond with questions, while affirmative phrases have a descending intonation.

Get the FREE VIDEO TRAINING at

http://www.lornavocals.com/p/speakoutbonus

Ascending ——>

1. You did?   Question

Descending ——>

2. You did!   Affirmation

Some people have a tendency to finish their statements with an ascending intonation. This might introduce a sense of doubt to your statements.

In order to deliver a powerful message, make sure that the intonation of your phrases is descending every time you finish an affirmative sentence.

Listen to the audio examples and exercises here:
http://www.lornavocals.com/p/speakoutbonus

In order to present yourself powerfully, you need to perform the words you are saying by incorporating vocal variations that reinforce the intention of your message.

PROLOGUE

So... What's next?

My goal with this book is to help you understand that the stage where your presentation skills are right now does not define you. Only after developing your potential with exercises and techniques, such as those I have mentioned in this book, will you have a better idea of your unexplored potential and how to take advantage of it.

If you have not done this yet, I strongly encourage you to access the free resources that I have prepared for you. Since we are talking about presentation skills, voice, and related topics, there is no better way for me to explain these subjects but teaching you on video. Once again, this is the link: http://www.lornavocals.com/p/speakoutbonus

However, if you really got the message, you are probably ready to take a step forward and start the actual training. I have prepared a special complete program with all the exercises you will need in order to develop your presentation skills. It includes dozens of hours of exercises on vocal technique, non-verbal communication, and word choice, while developing the

---

Get the FREE VIDEO TRAINING at

http://www.lornavocals.com/p/speakoutbonus

right mindset and staying connected to your mission and your audience in the most authentic way.

This is the SPEAK OUT! Online course, and it comes with awesome bonuses. You can sign up now and start your complete training right away: https://www.lornavocals.com/p/speak-out-sign-up

You can also have access to private training and workshops at corporate events. For more details, just send me an email at contact@lornavocal.com. I would love to know more about you and your experiences. Please feel free to contact me at any time.

Free your voice and become the best version of yourself. The world needs to hear!

Yours,

Lorna

Get the FREE VIDEO TRAINING at

http://www.lornavocals.com/p/speakoutbonus

BOOK LORNA EARNSHAW TO SPEAK

Book Lorna Earnshaw as your Keynote Speaker and you Are Guaranteed to Make your Event Inspirational, Educational, Motivational and Highly Entertaining!

Photo by Carlos Sillero

For more than two decades, Lorna Earnshaw has been on stage either as an international singer and dancer or as an educational speaker, inspiring and

---

Get the FREE VIDEO TRAINING at

http://www.lornavocals.com/p/speakoutbonus

instructing authors, performers, business owners, experts, consultants, and coaches.

Her unique style which combines her artistic skills, vocal technique and advanced branding and marketing strategies, inspires, empowers and entertains audiences while giving them the tools and strategies to grow in a personal and professional way.

Her keynote talks are delivered in English, Spanish, and Portuguese, according to the needs of every specific audience.

For more info and to book Lorna for your next event, email us at contact@lornavocal.com.

Get the FREE VIDEO TRAINING at
http://www.lornavocals.com/p/speakoutbonus

WILL YOU LEAVE A BOOK REVIEW?

Did you enjoy this book? I will be really grateful if you post a short review and your success story on Amazon right now!
I will really appreciate your support and I will consider all the reviews to improve my future publications.

To leave a review right now, go here:

www.lornavocals.com/p/speakoutreview

Get the FREE VIDEO TRAINING at

http://www.lornavocals.com/p/speakoutbonus

ABOUT THE AUTHOR

Lorna Earnshaw is a trilingual vocal coach, speaker, singer, songwriter and online marketing consultant based in Hollywood (CA). Of English descent, she graduated in Journalism in Argentina and got her Bachelor's Degree in Songwriting in Los Angeles. Lorna has been teaching vocals since 2003 and, in 2012, she released her own method in Portuguese, "Fundamentals of Vocal Technique". As of 2018, she has already helped more than 60,000 people free their voices through the Internet and more than 350 students in her private lessons. Her YouTube and Facebook accounts have more than 5 million video views altogether, while some of her posts have been seen more than 1.7 million times individually. She helps brands, artists and personalities to create a powerful presence on-camera, on-stage and during business meetings or keynotes, while she provides high-end training and consulting for companies and individuals. She also works as a songwriter, writing and recording songs in Portuguese and Spanish for Film and TV Hollywood productions.

Get the FREE VIDEO TRAINING at

http://www.lornavocals.com/p/speakoutbonus